So, you've bought my book or picked it up in the shop, thinking, 'what's this about?' Well, over the years of me making YouTube videos of my inventions, I've received so many emails from young people wanting to do what I do but not sure where to start.

This book is for those people who want to make stuff but need a little guidance. Even if you're familiar with hammers and saws, you'll still enjoy the invention projects in this book, as well as learning stuff about me and the cool things I've done. I've tried to make each project affordable and use materials everyone has access to, regardless of where they live. Each project will help you build on your skills and, when you finish the book, you should have enough knowledge and skills to tackle your own project ideas.

I'm sure you know this already, but it's really important you ask a grown-up to help you and make sure everything in this book is done with proper supervision and care. You never know – inventing might become your job one day, muhahaha!

Colin Furze

PUFFIN BOOKS

UK | USA | Canada | Ireland | Australia
India | New Zealand | South Africa

Puffin Books is part of the Penguin Random House group of companies
whose addresses can be found at global.penguinrandomhouse.com.

www.penguin.co.uk   www.puffin.co.uk   www.ladybird.co.uk

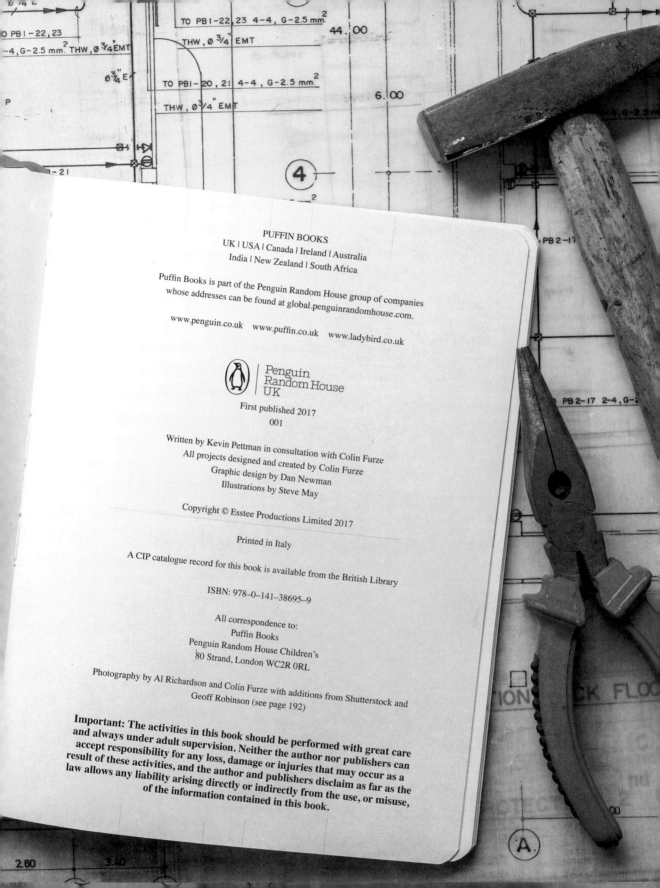 Penguin
Random House
UK

First published 2017
001

Written by Kevin Pettman in consultation with Colin Furze
All projects designed and created by Colin Furze
Graphic design by Dan Newman
Illustrations by Steve May

Printed in Italy

A CIP catalogue record for this book is available from the British Library

ISBN: 978–0–141–38695–9

All correspondence to:
Puffin Books
Penguin Random House Children's
80 Strand, London WC2R 0RL

Photography by Al Richardson and Colin Furze with additions from Shutterstock and
Geoff Robinson (see page 192)

**Important: The activities in this book should be performed with great care
and always under adult supervision. Neither the author nor publishers can
accept responsibility for any loss, damage or injuries that may occur as a
result of these activities, and the author and publishers disclaim as far as the
law allows any liability arising directly or indirectly from the use, or misuse,
of the information contained in this book.**

THIS BOOK ISN'T SAFE!

COLIN FURZE

PUFFIN

Contents

* I've made instructional videos for some of the inventions – scan this QR code or go to: www.puffin.co.uk/colin-furze

I'M COLIN FURZE!

That's right, it's me. Colin Furze. I'm a barmy bloke who loves building silly things, creating crazy inventions and generally having a laugh making stuff in my shed (aka The Shed). Millions of people watch my YouTube videos and subscribe to my channel. For some reason they enjoy watching me setting fire to things, making lots of noise, creating inventions that no one really needs and acting like a bit of an idiot!

Disclaimer: I am not an idiot. See page 16 where I even work out the square root of 113!

In *This Book Isn't Safe!* you'll discover all the cool things I've done in my 30-plus years on this planet. I'll tell you stacks of interesting, funny facts about myself, like my shoe size, my middle name and what my favourite food is.
Impressive, huh?

Only joking! There are waaaay more fun things than this in my book!

Oh, there's also the small matter of the **TEN TOTALLY COOL (AND BRAND-NEW) INVENTIONS I'LL SHOW YOU HOW TO BUILD!**
More of that in a bit, folks.

Some people call me a YouTuber, others think I'm an eccentric inventor, a mad scientist or a fruit cake who builds whacky machines in his shed. Truth is, I'm a bit of all these things.

FWOoOSH!!

Anyone can have fun bolting things, sticking things, bending things and bashing things using basic tools, techniques and materials. *This Book Isn't Safe!* shows you how to create **ten incredible inventions** with easy, step-by-step instructions. You don't have to be a genius or have loads of fancy gear to make these inventions; even if you've never held a screwdriver in your life, I'll reveal all you need to know. You'll soon be building brilliant (and crazy!) creations you've never even dreamed of!

MY YOUTUBE VIDEOS

I created a giant Star Wars AT-ACT (All Terrain Armored Cargo Transport) in my garden!

I dug a massive nuclear bunker under my back garden!

I built and rode a hoverbike using two paramotor engines!

I rode a toilet at over 50mph!

I built the world's fastest mobility scooter!

I set six Guinness World Records!

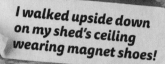

I walked upside down on my shed's ceiling wearing magnet shoes!

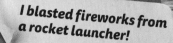

I blasted fireworks from a rocket launcher!

I made an Ejector Bed that flings you into the air!

I made the world's first jet-powered bicycle!

I created a 360° swing as tall as a house!

I designed shoes that vacuum the floor!

I invented slippers that are heated by flames!

I made a knife that cuts and toasts bread at the same time!

9

6 reasons why MY BOOK IS AWESOME!

1. YOU'LL MAKE THINGS

That's the whole point of *This Book Isn't Safe!* Whether you're eight or 88, I want you to start building my ten awesome inventions. You will need adult help along the way, but that's fine. Boys and girls, mums and dads, aunties, uncles and next-door neighbours can all get involved. Let's get the world building brilliant, bonkers creations!

2. IT'S GOT SECRET STUFF

You'll find out loads about me, and see some funny pictures from when I was younger. *This Book Isn't Safe!* is the first book I've ever made – I usually just scribble funny drawings and random words on to big bits of paper in my shed, like this . . .

3. IT'S FUNNY

If you've seen my YouTube videos, you'll know I like to have a laugh and a joke. I'm serious about building epic things, but I like to do it in a fun way. I've even written some jokes on pages 148-149.

WARNING! My jokes may be ultra lame!

4. IT'S NOT COMPLICATED

Hey, don't go thinking that the ten creations you'll build will be difficult or require you to have a degree in quantum physics and robotic engineering. I don't! Some of the materials you'll need include plastic milk bottles, a Frisbee and string. Simple stuff.

5. IT'S NOT BORING

I hate boring stuff, and my book is 100 per cent guaranteed not to be boring. Here's a picture of me pulling a funny face, just to demonstrate how completely un-boring my book is!

6. YOU CAN WRITE IN IT

Grab a pen and get scribblin'! Write ideas about what you want to build in the future at the end of the book, and even make notes on the other pages if you want. Go on – don't be scared to get your pen and pencil out!

! If this book isn't yours, if you've borrowed it or you're reading it in a bookshop, then DON'T write on it. That could get you into trouble.

STUFF ABOUT ME

Here goes. I was born in a lovely town called Stamford, in Lincolnshire, in the middle bit of England. I soon grew into a little boy, and I was quite a noisy, slightly cheeky chap. I have a sister called Ellie, and grew up having fun playing outside with my friends. Behind my house was a quarry, which became my adventure playground - I would build dens and play games with bits of wood and whatever else I could find there. It was brilliant fun.

Nowadays, a quarry is a good place to launch things!

I've always been pretty good on a computer.

One of my dens was this super high treehouse.

I was always interested in building stuff, and was very active (I couldn't sit still). I had a basic children's toolkit when I was about five or six and enjoyed putting wood together and bashing bits and pieces around. I also built lots of cars and machines with Meccano (simple building sets that contain small metal and plastic strips, nuts, bolts, rotors, wheels and whatever else). Meccano sets are fantastic.

I had a lot of LEGO (and no internet).

Back then, I liked TV shows like *Transformers*, which is still going now, and one called *Knight Rider*, which was about a talking car. My favourite birthday present was a model Dodge Charger car called General Lee from a show called *Dukes of Hazzard*. I still have that car now! I went to Malcolm Sargent Primary in Stamford and my school life was OK, although I did get a bit bored sometimes. I had to wear a tie to school, and I still wear one now when I show off my inventions on YouTube. I didn't like tucking my shirt into my trousers back then, and still don't tuck it in now. Some things never change, I guess!

I built a stunt ramp!

13

FURZE'S FACT FILE

Right, here's a bunch of random things you may be interested in knowing about me. That said, I'm sure there's one thing here you don't want to know . . .

Middle name: Peter

First job: I had a paper round when I was fourteen. I had it until I was eighteen, while I was training to be a plumber. I may have been the oldest paperboy in Lincolnshire!

Girlfriend's name: Charlotte

Fave TV show: *Formula One*. It's the only thing I'll watch at all costs, regardless of family events. I actually worried that my daughter, Erin, might've been born on a race day and I'd miss watching it!

Fave music band: Muse

Fave celebrity: Matt Bellamy, the lead singer and musician from Muse

Dream car: BMW M3

Best holiday: I went to Canada and got to mess about on snow with cars and machines (although I was filming as well, so it was a working holiday!)

Fave food: Roast dinner. Mmmm, lovely!

Worst food: Thai food. It's all a bit wet and spicy for me.

Best meal I can cook: Roast dinner. I love my roast dinners! I once created a Christmas Spinner Turkey-cooking Machine and cooked for Jamie Oliver!

Best mates: Rick Simpson (pictured right). He's the bloke who helps me in a lot of my videos. And Dave, who I met when we were building the local skatepark together.

Bedtime: About 11.30 p.m. to 12.00 a.m. If I go to bed too early I just lie there and can't sleep!

Biggest laugh: Stupid, silly and juvenile stuff makes me laugh. People falling over and mucking about, usually.

Musical instruments: I can't play any, but I'm teaching myself to play the drums.

Fave book: *This Book Isn't Safe!* obviously. But when I was young, I was fascinated by *How The Body Works*. I guess I've always wanted to know how things work – even my body!

Last time I farted in public: Er, I do occasionally – and always accidentally – let one go in meetings or something. It's usually when I bend down and one comes out. Sorry!*

Secret skill: I can work people out quite quickly when I first meet them. I think I'm quite intuitive.

Fave superhero: Magneto (he's the reason I made the magnet shoes!)

My superhero name would be: Palletto! I've made lots of things with wooden pallets – like a Wall of Death and the world's biggest bonfire.

*I said you might not want to know one of these facts!

NUMBER-CRUNCHIN' COLIN

It's time to get your calculator out and study these number-related stats and facts all about Mr Colin Furze (me!). Don't worry, I wasn't that keen on maths at school, so these pages are much more fun than working out the square root of 113 ...

The square root of 113 is 10.63.
(10.63 × 10.63 = 113. Well, 112.9969 actual(ly.)
I know this cos I goog(led it!

14/10/1979
My date of birth. Did you know I get a year older every time this date rolls round? Amazing!

26
Number of teeth that I have. (It's not easy to count them – you try it!) I lost a couple riding BMX bikes.

4
Do you like the ties that I wear on my YouTube videos? Well, I'm on my fourth one, as bad things happen to them eventually!

14
It's my fave number. I was born on 14 October, my son Jake was born on 14 September and my mum's birthday is 14 February. Weird, hey?!

176
That's how tall I am (in centimetres, obviously, not inches – that would make me taller than an African elephant).

2
That's the number of kids I have – Jake and little Erin. They make the same noise as about 27 kids, though.

0
I have a big, fat zero number of pets. But if I did get a dog I'd call it Gromit, after the cool dog from *Wallace & Gromit*.

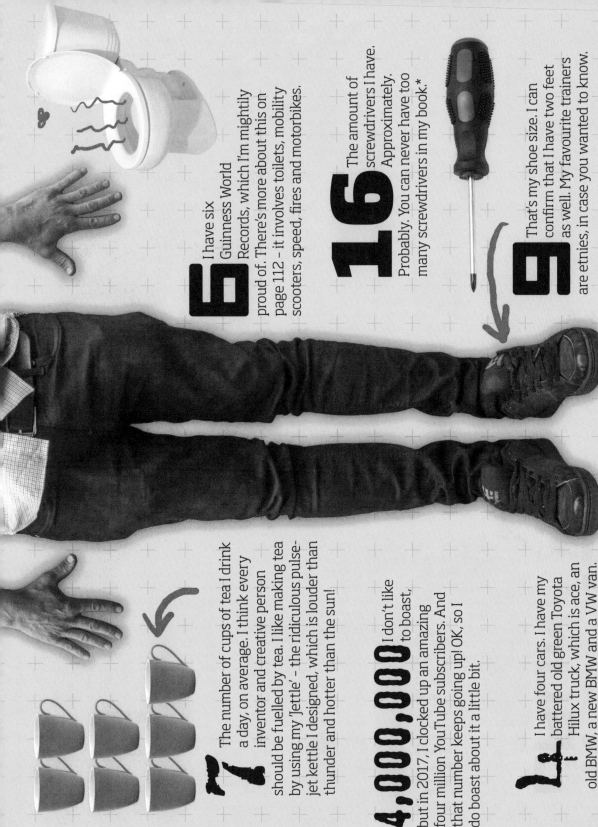

6

I have six Guinness World Records, which I'm mightily proud of. There's more about this on page 112 – it involves toilets, mobility scooters, speed, fires and motorbikes.

16

The amount of screwdrivers I have. Approximately. Probably. You can never have too many screwdrivers in my book.*

9

That's my shoe size. I can confirm that I have two feet as well. My favourite trainers are etnies, in case you wanted to know.

*In my book' is just an expression. Please note that there are not sixteen screwdrivers actually in this book.

7

The number of cups of tea I drink a day, on average. I think every inventor and creative person should be fuelled by tea. I like making tea by using my 'Jettle' – the ridiculous pulse-jet kettle I designed, which is louder than thunder and hotter than the sun!

4,000,000

I don't like to boast, but in 2017 I clocked up an amazing four million YouTube subscribers. And that number keeps going up! OK, so I do boast about it a little bit.

4

I have four cars. I have my battered old green Toyota Hilux truck, which is ace, an old BMW, a new BMW and a VW van.

PEANUT BUTTER SANDWICHES & CATS

That's definitely the strangest title in my book! But don't worry, the peanut butter and cats don't go together. That would be gross.

My mum made me **peanut butter sandwiches** for school packed lunch. I'm a very fussy eater and I had peanut butter sarnies every day for about ten years!

Cats were a big thing in my life as a young boy. My mum adopted cats, which meant our house always had loads of furry little fellas running around. Some of the cats liked sleeping on my bed, and one day I came home from school to find that a cat had given birth to kittens on my bed! Mum made me sleep in my sister's bedroom until the kittens could leave their mother. Ugh! Sharing a room with your sister!

meowww

Once, in the school canteen, I remember mucking around with my friend. He had cucumber sandwiches and we hatched a plan to chuck my peanut butter up to the ceiling, then throw cucumber up and stick it to the peanut butter. **It worked!** We did it every day for ages until there was stinky cucumber and peanut butter spread all over the ceiling. But one day we were caught in the act by a teacher. He wasn't happy when he saw the smeared and splattered ceiling. We got in trouble for it, but it was mega funny!

BUILDING, BMX BIKES AND BEDROOMS...

Even when I became a teenager (which I can confirm happened on my thirteenth birthday), I still loved messing around at the quarry near my house, building tree houses, underground dens and contraptions with anything I could get my hands on. The trouble was that my dad wouldn't let me in his shed to build things at home, which meant I often had to use my bedroom. It wasn't ideal, but I had a little lathe machine, a vice and all sorts of tools in there – I was just desperate to make things. It was madness really, and I'm surprised I didn't fall through the floor because of all the vibrations the machines made!

I've got a bigger lathe now, and a proper shed to put it in . . .

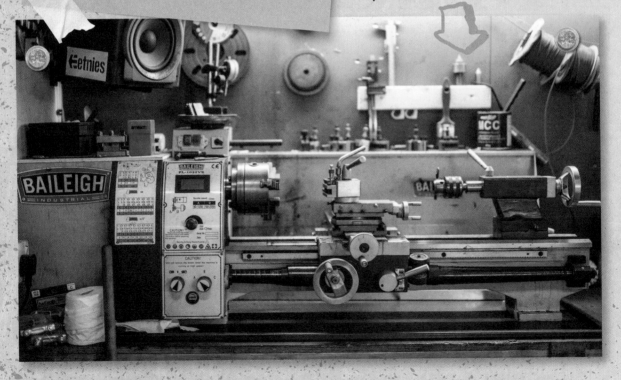

When I was about fifteen, I bought an old Raleigh Burner BMX bike for ten quid. My mate also had one, and we were going to use both to make a cool go-kart. But then we started riding our BMX bikes around and suddenly I really got into BMXing! I enjoyed flat-land riding – which is when you do tricks and stunts – but I didn't do much dirt jumping on big ramps as I injured my knee doing that. I won a few amateur BMX competitions so I must have been OK at it!

me!

It wasn't until many years later, when my dad sadly died, that I was able to get into his shed and use the benches and the space. That was a big moment for me and I could take my tools out of my bedroom.

Speaking of bedrooms (again!), it was while I was sitting in a friend's bedroom staring at a radiator when I was sixteen that I had the idea to become a plumber when I left school.

RIGHT, that's enough about me – time for you lot to get building stuff! WOOHOO!

Turn the page to start making cool inventions!

CONCRETE-CRUSHER WELLIES

You might nee to try this a couple of times to get it right.

Yep. The first things we're going to make together are CONCRETE-CRUSHER WELLIES! The name reveals everything here: they're basically a pair of concrete wellington boots that will crush things. Simple. They are 100 per cent fun, 100 per cent silly, 100 per cent easy to make and 78.2 per cent* practical in everyday life!

*This practicality rating is just an estimate, of course!

Use strong thick bags, not flimsy ones!

WHAT WILL YOU NEED?

- ⚙ A pair of wellington boots. These can be old wellies and don't have to match. Make sure your feet fit in them easily, though. You'll also want a left and a right boot.

- ⚙ A bag of ready-made cement – preferably stuff that you only need to add water to, as that's the easiest to mix. Most DIY stores sell it and a 10kg bag should be enough.

- ⚙ Two plastic carrier bags.

- ⚙ A strong piece of wood or a wooden spoon.

- ⚙ An old bucket and rubber gloves.

- ⚙ Kitchen roll and duct tape.

- ⚙ Two cardboard tubes.

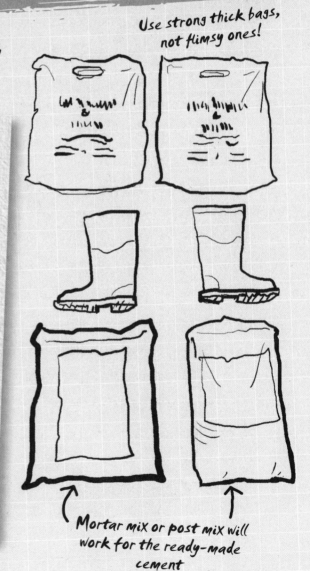

Mortar mix or post mix will work for the ready-made cement

ADULT SUPERVISION!
Imagine that if by 'supervision' I meant an adult with super vision – who could see through walls or had optical X-ray powers! What I mean is, you need an adult to help you make the inventions and check you're wearing the right safety clothing, like goggles or gloves.

CONCRETE AND CEMENT: WHAT'S THE DIFFERENCE?

You may be a bit confused – this invention is called Concrete-crusher Wellies, but you've mixed cement. Are concrete and cement the same thing? Without getting too boring, cement is a part of concrete – concrete is made of cement, sand, aggregates like stone, and even bits of metal and other fibres.

WHAT ARE THE BOOTS FOR?

Isn't it obvious? No? Well, when you've made them, these big boots will be brill for bashing and banging and breaking bits and bobs to pieces. Blimey, I've never written so many words beginning with B in all my life! These boots can be used to crush plastic and card before you put it in the recycling bin, or even to break up broken old toys. Bonkers! (Another B-word!)

WHAT'S FOR TEA TONIGHT?

Huh?! Sorry, this question shouldn't be here. (I just suddenly wondered what I'd be having for tea later on!*)

*It was baked beans on toast, in case you wanted to know.

TOP TIP!
Using boots that are slightly too big for you is a good idea, because then your feet will fit in them easily when the cement has dried.

STEP 1

Grab your cardboard tubes and cut off four sections that are 3cm deep. Tape two sections to the bottom of each boot. Something like duct tape will hold them. Having card stuck here means the cement can go under each boot.

STEP 2

Open the bag of cement and follow the instructions for how to mix it with water in your bucket. Use half of the mixture. Find a piece of wood or an old wooden spoon to stir it. The cement should be as thick as possible, with just the right amount of water.

STEP 3

Stick one boot in the middle of one carrier bag. Start placing the mixed cement around the foot of the boot. If you're using a wooden spoon, use that to get the cement in, or you could use your hands to lift it in. **Wear rubber gloves!**

TOP TIP!

Stuff some kitchen roll or a small towel down in the boot. This helps the boot keep its shape and stops cement falling inside.

STEP 4

Start to shape the cement around the boot and make it look like a shoe. You could place bricks or heavy tins on either side to help. Make sure the mixture goes all around the boot and underneath it.

STEP 5

When that boot is done, take the remaining unmixed cement, mix it as before and make the other concrete boot in the same way.

Smooth the top edge as the concrete sets

STEP 6

Leave both cemented boots outside overnight to set. If it's going to be frosty, leave them in a garage or shed.

TOP TIP!

A 10kg bag of cement should make enough for two boots, but it will depend on the size of your boots.

STEP 7

Early the next day, it's a good idea to carefully poke a few holes with scissors in the side of each carrier bag around the mixture. This will help the water dry out properly.

STEP 8

Later in the day, if the mixture has dried and is solid (it may need longer to fully set) you will be able to peel the bag away and your Concrete-crusher Wellies are complete!

Paint them if you like!

> *You've made your first invention! Do a little Colin Furze celebratory dance!*

How much fun was that?! I'm sure you had a laugh mixing your cement, getting the thickness of it just right and then shaping it around each boot. You may have needed to try this a couple of times to get it right, but that's fine - people rarely get things perfect the first time they try something new.

HAIR WE GO!

When you're mixing your cement, there are also some things you can add to it to make it even stronger …

Hair

Short human hair is perfect for helping to bind the mixture together. The short fibres mix brilliantly. Ask your hairdresser for a bag of the stuff after your next visit (probably best to stick with your own, though, and make sure they are short as short fibres work best!).

Small screws and nails

If you have any old screws or nails, chuck some of these in your bucket when you're mixing the cement.

Wool

Not bundles of wool from a knitting bag! But if you live near fields or farms, there's often bits of sheep's wool stuck to wire fences and the like. Use this in your mixture and it'll help strengthen it.

COLIN'S CHALLENGE!
What else do you think could be added to cement to boost its power? Note: Weetabix and chewing gum are no good!

CRUSH! CRUSH! STOMP! SMASH!

THINGS YOU CAN CRUSH:

* Empty plastic milk bottles
* Empty cans
* Cardboard boxes
* Broken old toys
* Flowers in the garden

Actually no!!!! Don't crush your parents' plants. Try sticks instead!

I'll be rating each invention in this book, based on three main areas: strength, detail and difficulty. Each rating is on a scale from one to ten. Strength refers to how tough the final product is, and detail to how detailed it is to make – ten being the hardest. Difficulty refers to how complex it is to make. As you can see, the Concrete-crusher Wellies are super easy to make!

••RATING••

STRENGTH:
DETAIL:
DIFFICULTY:

INVENTING STUFF IS COOL!

I like to think I make and invent things that no one else would bother to . . . because my ideas are just too ridiculous. My inventions usually have a purpose, like heated slippers to keep your feet toasty, but no one would actually try to sell them in a shop. They might just set fire to your trousers, which is not a good outcome.

Having the power to think, **Right, today I'll invent a machine that fires cake into my mouth at top speed** is quite special. (See the Cake-O-Matic on page 82!) I know that makes my job pretty awesome. If people didn't invent things and take their ideas from scribbled bits of paper through to build stage, then the world would be worse off. OK, so I come up with silly stuff and show off in The Shed, but other, more serious inventors actually design practical things. Apparently James Dyson, the bloke who made the Dyson vacuum, had 5,127 prototypes before he finally nailed exactly how it would work. I never wake up in the morning and think that I can't be bothered to build things or invent ways to make something work - especially not when I'm fired from my mattress by my Ejector Bed!

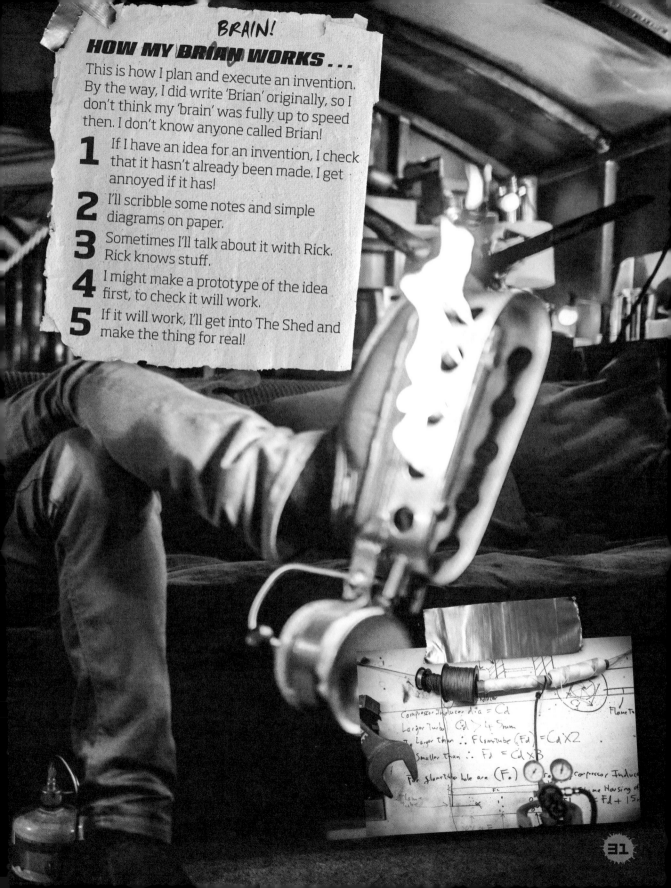

BRAIN!

HOW MY BRIAN WORKS . . .

This is how I plan and execute an invention. By the way, I did write 'Brian' originally, so I don't think my 'brain' was fully up to speed then. I don't know anyone called Brian!

1 If I have an idea for an invention, I check that it hasn't already been made. I get annoyed if it has!

2 I'll scribble some notes and simple diagrams on paper.

3 Sometimes I'll talk about it with Rick. Rick knows stuff.

4 I might make a prototype of the idea first, to check it will work.

5 If it will work, I'll get into The Shed and make the thing for real!

WHAT'S THE WORLD'S BEST INVENTION?

BICYCLE

It's the bicycle, definitely. I don't think you can fault the bike as the world's best invention in any of its forms, either as a bicycle or a motorbike. Obviously I have some history here, being a big BMX fan as a teenager and having made jet-powered bicycles and mega-long motorbikes! But young people all over the world love to ride bikes and often that develops into a passion for motorbikes or other things with wheels.

This doesn't include shopping trollies!

On a bike, you can do pretty much anything. With basic and inexpensive maintenance, a simple bike will last a lifetime. You can ride around the world on a bike, and motorbikes will pretty much go anywhere – up mountains, across deserts. Some bloke even surfed waves riding a motorbike!

I rode a bike with ice wheels on a Canadian glacier. Because I could.

PIPE SLICE

One of the best bits of kit for a plumber. After you've used one of these to cut a copper pipe once, using a hacksaw to do the same thing is a total chore. Admittedly, it is of no use to anyone apart from for, er, slicing a pipe in two, but this little device has such a clever and neat design. Brilliant.

PHILLIPS SCREWDRIVER

This is a very neat, but very simple idea, and it makes screwing screws soooo much easier! A Phillips screwdriver has a slotted tip, with one indent running vertically and one horizontally. This matches the two slots on a screw's head and means it's much easier to turn the screw. An old screw had just one slot. You'll use a screwdriver later in my book and will discover how easy it is.

iPHONE

It seems an obvious choice, and it annoys me how iPhone users have to keep updating their software, but think about the impact Apple's super-smart phone has had. It launched in 2007 and over one billion have been sold since. It paved the way for touchscreens, apps, WiFi, social media on mobile devices and much more. Will it be the biggest invention of the 21st century?

I sent a mobile phone over 100,000 feet into space, attached to a weather balloon, and watched the recordings when it came back to earth!

THE SINCLAIR C5 ELECTRIC VEHICLE

Not everything that's ever been invented has been a massive success. I hate carrot-flavoured ice cream, for example. But one of the worst inventions I can think of is the Sinclair C5 electric vehicle. This battery-powered car-bike thingy was released in 1985 and invented by a British bloke called Clive Sinclair. Now, Clivey boy had already invented some great computers at that time and they'd been very successful, but the C5 was an absolute flop. Sinclair stopped building them just a few months after they first arrived!

There were a few problems: the battery wasn't great, it struggled to get up hills, it had an eventual top speed of just 15mph, going round corners was tough and, as riders were low down, they weren't always seen by other cars on the road. Bit dangerous, that. I've actually driven a C5 and it was terrible!

Luckily I had the chance to tinker with a Sinclair C5 vehicle. When I appeared on *Gadget Geeks*, a Sky TV show, a few years back, I was challenged to 'improve' a C5. I came up with a C5 monster-truck design, which had three huge wheels, a petrol engine that reached 40mph and a ride height of about 1.5 metres. It was a bit wobbly to drive, but much more fun than the original. I don't reckon my design would sell half the amount that even Clive managed with his vehicles in the 1980s, though!

MY SLIGHTLY RUBBISH INVENTIONS...

I made an Instant Bacon-cooking Machine. The bacon slid through the rollers, got stuck and didn't cook enough.

Tea2Me!
Move a cup of tea about 10cm, very slowly. No, I don't know why, either!

Jetwipe!
Unroll some toilet paper at very high speed, using a painfully noisy pulse-jet.

BRRMM!

WHICH TYPE OF INVENTOR ARE YOU?

Imagine you are a full-time, professional inventor. Play this fun game to reveal what you'd be like - just choose your answer and follow the arrow after each question.

WHITE COAT

When you show off your inventions, do you like wearing a white coat, a beige-brown shirt and tie, or are you not bothered?

NOT BOTHERED

START

Would you rather invent something that's practical and will make you a billionaire, or something that's silly and will make everyone laugh?

PRACTICAL

SHIRT AND TIE

ZER

How many world records have you set? A big fat zero or a mega amazing six?

LAUGH

SIX

Do you prefer concocting things with test tubes or messing about on YouTube?

TEST TUBES

MAD SCIENTIST

It looks like you're great at making practical things while wearing a scientist's laboratory coat. Just be careful with those test tubes in the lab!

YOUTUBE

Is it best that your creations work properly and quietly, or properly and LOUDLY?

QUIETLY

MASTER BUILDER

You love quietly making top-quality inventions that work really well. You're not bothered about what you wear, or about setting world records – you're just a master of your trade!

NO

LOUDLY

If you were an inventor, could your name be an anagram of Zircon Fuel?

Zircon Fuel? Sounds like something used to power a spaceship! Coool!!

YES

MINI MR FURZE

That's right – you're just like me! You want to invent silly things (that are a bit practical) while wearing a shirt and tie, and while being very LOUD on YouTube!

37

ESSENTIAL INVENTOR'S KIT

You've now discovered which type of inventor you are (hopefully you're a Mini Mr Furze!) and it's about time you know which essential bits of kit, gear and tools you'll need as an inventor-creator-builder-type person. *This Book Isn't Safe!* is all about using basic materials and techniques as much as possible, but there are some things you'll definitely have to get your hands on . . .

SCREWDRIVER

You didn't need one to make the Concrete-crusher Wellies, but most of the other inventions need a screwdriver. Ask an adult if you can use/borrow/politely steal their screwdrivers and you'll find most of them have more than they actually need! I explained what a Phillips screwdriver is on page 33. You'll also need a 'flathead' screwdriver, which has a tip like this . . .

Handy for: screwing in screws, which I talk about on pages 64-65.

Phillips

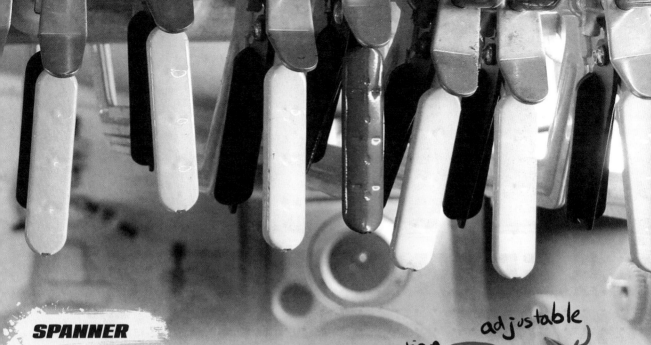

SPANNER

Spanners come in lots of sizes, with big or small openings. They aren't too expensive, but again see if you can borrow the ones you'll need. A combination spanner has an open C-shape at one end and a ring at the other. An adjustable spanner is a spanner that you can make the C-shaped opening smaller or larger on – you won't need as many different-sized individual spanners, but adjustable spanners are heavier and bigger.

Handy for: tightening and loosening different-sized nuts and bolts.

combination

adjustable

HACKSAW AND SAW

Surely you've seen a saw? Maybe you've seen a saw while sitting on a seesaw by the seashore?! Ha ha! A junior hacksaw is the name given to a smaller hacksaw and has an individual strip of sharp metal teeth. A junior hacksaw is good for sawing through small bits of wood and metal. A regular hacksaw is bigger but has the same shape and design. A normal saw has a larger metal blade and can come in different sizes.

Handy for: cutting wood and metal.

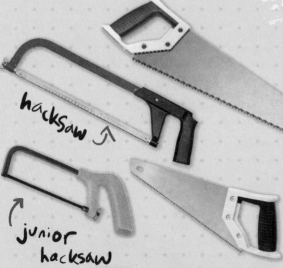

hacksaw

junior hacksaw

POWER DRILL

I'll show you how to safely use a power drill to make a pilot hole on pages 46-47. A power drill lets you make quick and accurate holes in wood so that you can screw a screw into the hole. Simple and basic drills may cost around £20, but ask an adult if you can use their drill (a much cheaper option!).
Handy for: drilling holes.

TAPE MEASURE

Think of this as a massive, bendy ruler that you can keep in your pocket.
Handy for: measuring things, like wood*, and for finding the centre of objects.

* It's also fun to measure the longest crisp in each crisp packet you eat. The longest crisp I've measured was a mighty 7.4cm!

TOP TIP!

The majority of the equipment you'll need to build my ten inventions can be bought from local DIY shops. Sometimes you'll need to buy things on the internet though, particularly electrical bits for the Auto Dart-blaster Firing System and the Remote-control Hosepipe Pranker. Objects like the washing line pulleys and picture frame corners can also be bought cheaply from websites. You must have adult supervision when you purchase any products via the internet.

TZZZZ

OTHER BITS AND PIECES

You'll need some screws to build many of the inventions in *This Book Isn't Safe!* These will mainly be screws for going into wood and will be of different sizes. My advice is to ask a grown-up for a load of their spare screws.

Nuts, bolts and washers A bolt is like a long, thick screw (without a point on the end) that secures objects together. Nuts and washers on the ends of bolts help hold them in place.

Cable ties are quite handy and are something I use on the Auto Dart-blaster Firing System and the Bike-wheel Fire Vortex. You may also be able to use them on some other inventions. A cable tie is a thin piece of plastic that neatly hooks into itself to secure or tie an object.

Tape Sometimes I'll refer to electrical tape, masking tape, black tape or gaffer tape.

Screw eyes This isn't when you roll your eyes in your head! A screw eye is a metal hook with a screw on the end.

TECHNIQUES & TIPS

Now then, I'm not assuming that all of you reading my book already know how to saw wood, drill metal, strip wire and so on.

Some of you may have experience of this, or perhaps you've seen others doing it, which is great. But even if you think a pilot hole is something a person flying a plane looks through, or if you've only ever heard a drill while sitting in your dentist's chair, I'll explain all the techniques and tips you'll need to help you build all the inventions!

oooh!

Don't worry about these techniques being tough to do. Given the right tools, time to practise and a few tips, any of us can drill through metal, for example. When I was a lad I learned some stuff from my dad, and I also practised safely screwing screws into wood, learning how to cut wire with pliers, drilling a counter-sunk hole and doing loads of other fun things.

As human beings, we don't know how to do anything until we're taught it and given time to pack it all into our brainboxes. You're going to make the odd mistake as you build things, but that's normal and part of the process of learning new things. Learn from your mistakes, that's what I say!

grrrr

STUFF YOU'LL LEARN TO DO

Sawing wood
I can do this ☐
I can't do this (yet!) ☐

Drilling wood
I can do this ☐
I can't do this (yet!) ☐

Measuring
I can do this ☐
I can't do this (yet!) ☐

Screwing screws
I can do this ☐
I can't do this (yet!) ☐

Tightening nuts
I can do this ☐
I can't do this (yet!) ☐

Sawing metal
I can do this ☐
I can't do this (yet!) ☐

Drilling metal
I can do this ☐
I can't do this (yet!) ☐

Stripping wire
I can do this ☐
I can't do this (yet!) ☐

Connecting wire
I can do this ☐
I can't do this (yet!) ☐

Joining wood with bolts
I can do this ☐
I can't do this (yet!) ☐

Joining metal with bolts
I can do this ☐
I can't do this (yet!) ☐

How to:
SAW WOOD

ADULT SUPER VISION NEEDED

Pay attention, Furze fans - I'm about to explain some of the simple techniques you need to know to help you make the inventions in this book. Here, you'll learn how to saw. You 'wood' not believe how fun and easy it is after a bit of practice!

1 Use a saw with a big metal blade. A hacksaw will cut wood, but it's not as good.

2 Make a line with a pencil showing where you need to saw. Don't just make one or two pencil marks.

3 Saw on a workbench or a slightly raised surface. You can't put wood on the floor and cut it, cos your saw will be at the wrong angle and the blade will hit the ground.

TOP TIP!
You can carefully press a finger against the blade (well away from the teeth) as a guide to help you make your first few cuts.

4 Have the biggest part of the wood against your workbench and keep your line hanging just over the edge. Use the hand you're not sawing with to press the large part down. You could also use your knee to hold it down.

5 Hold the middle of the saw's blade at the start of your pencil line, with the saw at an angle of about 60°. Pull the saw back towards you very slowly.

TOP TIP!
Practise sawing bits of old wood before you start cutting pieces that you'll need for your inventions.

6 Carefully take the saw out of the tiny groove you've just cut and place the middle of the blade back in the groove, as in step 5. Slowly pull the saw towards you again and repeat three or four times. You want to make a small cut a few millimetres deep.

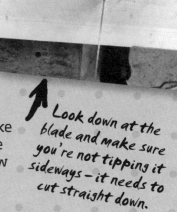

7 When you have this tiny cut, you can move the saw backwards and forward, in a smooth and slow movement, and saw through the wood. Take your time, concentrate and make sure you saw along the line.

Look down at the blade and make sure you're not tipping it sideways – it needs to cut straight down.

8 Just before you finish, slow down and ask someone to hold the piece that would fall to the ground. You don't want this wood to drop, as it could splinter the wood. If you're supporting the big end of the wood with your knee, you could use your free hand to catch the piece that comes off.

Oh no!

ADULT SUPER VISION NEEDED

How to:
DRILL WOOD

You'll have seen me whacking a drill into wood on my YouTube videos. I've done it thousands of times, but you may have never used a drill. That's no problem. Here's your handy guide.

1 This is a typical drill. Often it's called a power drill or a cordless drill if it has a battery and no cable or plug on the end.

2 Read the drill's instruction manual to understand how to attach a drill bit. Or ask an adult to show you. The drill bit attaches to the drill and makes the hole in the wood you drill.

3 Always measure and mark with a pencil on the wood the exact spot you need to drill. Never just guess!

TOP TIP!

If you can, put the wood into a vice, or clamp it to your bench, to stop it from moving. If you're working on a surface, place a piece of scrap wood underneath so you don't damage the surface.

4 Hold the drill at an upright angle, pull the trigger and use a little pressure to push the drill down into the wood. You don't need to be Superman or Superwoman – let the drill do the work and move it slowly. Don't wiggle the drill around.

5 When you've drilled the hole, keep your finger on the trigger to keep the drill going and slowly pull the drill up and out of the hole. If you drill down, then stop the drill and try to pull it out, you'll find that it'll be stuck.

6 Don't drill too close to the edge of a piece of wood, because you'll probably split the wood. Also, try to avoid the knots. Knots are the dark spots that appear in wood.

TOP TIP! Practise drilling holes in scrap pieces of wood until you're happy using a drill.

7 Later, I'll ask you to drill 'pilot holes' in wood. This means you're drilling a hole that you can then screw a screw into. If you don't drill a pilot hole first, the screw will probably split and crack the wood. (On pages 64-65 I'll explain about pilot holes and screw size.)

8 Counter sinking is a clever thing. You'll need a countersink drill bit. This will make a wide hole on the wood's surface so that the screw head fits into it. It makes the screw look neat and means the screw head doesn't rub against anything else.

How to:
MEASURE

Have you ever heard the expression 'How long's a piece of string'? Well, if you can measure properly, you'll be able to answer that!

Here's a piece of string - measure it now and write the answer here:

A tape measure and a ruler are the two things you'll need for measuring when you make the inventions in my book. A ruler is good because it has a straight edge that you can draw a pencil line alongside easily.

Plastic rulers are absolutely fine, but you might know someone who has a steel or metal ruler you could borrow. These are obviously tougher and less likely to get bashed up as you build stuff!

A tape measure is handy for measuring distances longer than your ruler. Hook the end of it over the start of the object you want to measure, like the edge of a piece of wood, pull it along, and the tape will come out showing the distance in centimetres.

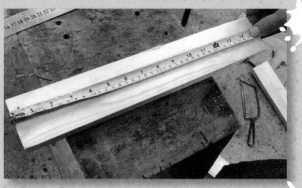

1 You can lock a tape measure by flicking the switch near your finger. This will stop the tape from getting longer or shorter. When you unlock it, the tape will quickly roll back in, so be careful it doesn't hit your fingers!

2 Always use a sharp pencil to mark the length of something. If you make a fat, squidgy mark with a felt pen, for example, your measuring won't be as accurate.

TOP TIP!
Use a calculator to work out measurements if it helps. Phones and tablets have a calculator on them too, remember.

3 Double check all your measuring before you cut wood with a saw. If you measure incorrectly and make something too small, you'll be in a bit of bother!

To mark straight across a bit of wood, use a set square . . . or the handle of your saw.

Do you need a long ruler? How about Queen Victoria?! Ha ha!

TOP TIP!
Practise measuring things around your house with a tape measure, such as the kitchen table, the height of the doors and the length of your parents!

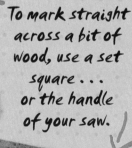

BRILLIANT BEDROOM-TIDY PULLEY

I've already said there's nothing boring in this book. In fact, these pages are packed with boredom-busting builds and projects! Let's agree on one thing that's utterly, utterly boring: having to tidy your bedroom. It's right up there with watching paint dry! But what if you could create a slick device that instantly swept your bedroom floor clean? Well, step back and behold the Brilliant Bedroom-tidy Pulley!

WHAT WILL YOU NEED?

- ⚙ Tape measure and pencil.

- ⚙ Two plastic milk bottles. Make sure they're empty.

- ⚙ A large piece of thick wood. You can buy a piece from a DIY shop, but first see if there's some wood around your house or in your garden or shed that you can reuse.

- ⚙ About 6 or 7 metres of cord or string. Cord will be better, as it's less likely to snag, but string or thin rope is fine, too.

- ⚙ Two screw eyes. Here's a picture of what a screw eye looks like – it's a shiny, screwy thing with a rounded hook.

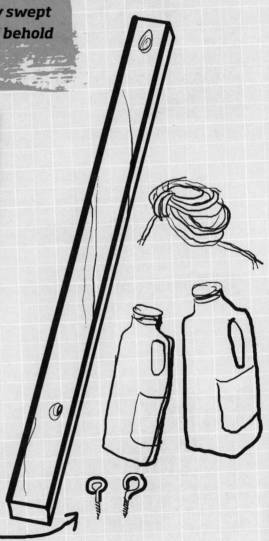

WHAT DOES IT DO?

The Brilliant Bedroom-tidy Pulley tidies your bedroom floor in seconds. Once the invention is in place and the plastic milk bottles are attached to two of your bed legs, you just pull the string and the pulley cleverly sweeps everything on your carpet under your bed. Your parents will be shocked by how quickly your room is tidied!

GREAT FOR TIDYING:
* Building bricks all over the floor
* Toys thrown on the carpet
* Dirty socks lying around

'ADULT SUPER VISION NEEDED

NOT SO GREAT FOR:
* Cats. If your poor pet is sleeping on your bedroom carpet, it's gonna get a fright when you unleash the Brilliant Bedroom-tidy Pulley!

That's the second time I've mentioned cats in a bedroom!

STEP 1

Take a tape measure and measure the length of your bed from the headboard to the end. If you don't have a tape measure, use a ruler by marking the end of the ruler with your finger, then move the ruler along to where your finger is. Repeat this until you've measured your bed.

STEP 2

Using the sawing technique from pages 44–45, cut a piece of wood the same length as your bed. Ideally, this wood needs to be about 5- or 6cm thick, so that it has enough weight to move whatever's on your floor.

Sand the edges smooth!

TOP TIP!

If the wood starts to split when you're twisting the screw eye into the hole, you may need to drill a slightly bigger pilot hole.

STEP 3

Drill a small pilot hole about 2cm from each end of the wood, roughly in the middle of the wood. Take a screw eye and slowly twist one into each hole.

STEP 4

Now you'll need your plastic milk bottles. Carefully cut a hole with scissors in each bottle, roughly the same size and shape as a leg of your bed. You can measure the width or circumference of one leg and draw it with a pen on the bottle.

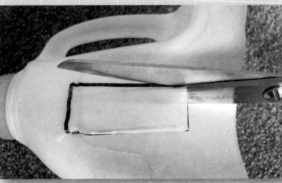

STEP 5

The hole you cut should be quite near to where the plastic handle is. You only need to cut one hole in each carton.

TOP TIP!

You can cut off the part of the milk bottle you're not using, so that it doesn't take up space under your bed.

STEP 6

Ask an adult to help you lift up the long side of your bed so that you can slip the empty milk bottles under the two raised legs. Each leg should fit nicely into the holes you've cut.

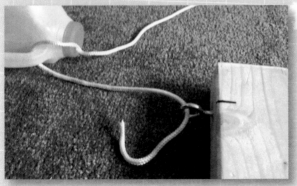

STEP 7

With the bottles firmly fixed under your bed legs, thread your rope or string through each screw eye on the wood. Then put one end through the milk-bottle handle on the same side as the screw eye. Repeat on the other side. Look at this little scribble, just in case you're a bit confused!

STEP 8

Move the piece of wood out away from your bed, but keep it in line with your bed. With both ends of the rope in your hands, pull the rope and the Brilliant Bedroom-tidy Pulley will move towards you and sweep whatever's in front of it neatly under your bed! You'll never waste hours picking stuff up from your floor again!

TOP TIP!

You may need to stand up on your bed when you pull the string or rope in, just so that you have enough room and power to sweep everything up.

LAZY TIP!

You could just tie the string to each end of the wood and not use screw eyes, but this may mean the wood doesn't move so smoothly across the floor.

You could see if the pulley works better on the legs nearer to the wall.

54

'ROOM' FOR IMPROVEMENT

*Get it? 'Room' for improvement, as in bed**room**? Anyway, there's lots more you can do with this clever tidying device and ways that you can make it even cooler. You should think of it as a giant bulldozer, clearing away everything in your bedroom in its path!*

3 FUN FURZEY IDEAS

⚙ Have you seen those rubber draft seals or brushes that are attached to the bottom of doors? If you have any of this stuff lying around in your garage or shed, then you could attach it to the bottom of the wood. This will help scoop up even *more* things from the floor.

⚙ Cut a strip of cardboard the same length as the wood and the same height as the gap under your bed. Staple, glue or tape the cardboard to the wood. When the wood is pulled in, you'll hide the mess under your bed.

⚙ Try painting the piece of wood to make it look extra cool in your bedroom. You could disguise it by making it the same colour as your floor - then your cat will get an extra big shock when it suddenly moves towards it!

COLIN'S CHALLENGE!
Where else could you use an invention like this? Would it work under the legs of the sofa in the lounge, perhaps?

??

••RATING••

STRENGTH: ⚙⚙⚙⚙⚙⚙⚙⚙⚙⚙⚙

DETAIL: ⚙⚙⚙⚙⚙⚙⚙⚙⚙⚙⚙

DIFFICULTY: ⚙⚙⚙⚙⚙⚙⚙⚙⚙⚙⚙

YEP, I USED TO BE A PLUMBER!

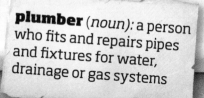

plumber (*noun*): a person who fits and repairs pipes and fixtures for water, drainage or gas systems

I looked up the word 'plumber' in a dictionary and this is what it said. Pretty spot on, that.

When I left school, I always knew I wanted to do a job with my hands, which could have meant being a builder or an electrician, but plumbing it was.

I trained for three years to be a plumber. It should've taken four years, but I found it quite easy. I went to college one day a week and worked for a company in Stamford for the other four, learning on the job. My mate Rick, who appears in lots of my YouTube videos now, actually trained me and we worked together for years.

I was a very good plumber and loved fixing things for people and making them happy after, say, their heating had broken or a tap was leaking. It sounds boring, but I quite liked it. Working in an office or in front of a computer all day would have been a nightmare for me. I was a full-time plumber until I was about 31, but by then my YouTube channel was taking off and I decided to put my plumbing tools away for good. That said, if I had to be a plumber again one day I'd happily go back to it.

WORST THINGS 'ABOUT PLUMBING . . .

* Working in lofts — they're full of itchy insulation and spiders!
* Unblocking toilet drains
* My work-mates hung me out of a window once!

BEST THINGS 'ABOUT PLUMBING . . .

* Working with my mate Rick!
* It taught me lots of techniques and tricks
* Unblocking toilet drains (weirdly, there's a big sense of satisfaction in it, but it's also on the worst things too, of course!)

Since you don't pronounce the B in plumber and plumbing, it should really be 'plummer' and 'plumming', I reckon.
Just a thought!

ME AND YOUTUBE

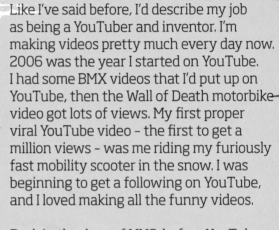

Like I've said before, I'd describe my job as being a YouTuber and inventor. I'm making videos pretty much every day now. 2006 was the year I started on YouTube. I had some BMX videos that I'd put up on YouTube, then the Wall of Death motorbike video got lots of views. My first proper viral YouTube video – the first to get a million views – was me riding my furiously fast mobility scooter in the snow. I was beginning to get a following on YouTube, and I loved making all the funny videos.

Back in the days of VHS, before YouTube and computers, making videos was such hard work for me. I had to use two video recorders (I didn't have a computer), and if I made a mistake it just had to go in the video. The picture and sound quality were pretty bad, too. It wasn't until a few years later that I was able to use a laptop to edit, and that was an absolute godsend for me! Editing my videos on computer was right up there with passing my driving test and getting my first welding machine – key points in my life! Suddenly, I could move bits of the video around, shoot much more stuff and speed the whole process up.

YouTube in London sends me fantastic awards each time my channel reaches another million subscribers. In 2016, I got one for having four million subscribers!

I got my own shed in 2010, and that meant I had a permanent place to film all of my videos. They began to look more professional and I became better at making them. I also read the suggestions that people were leaving in my comments sections about what people wanted me to do and build.

In 2011, I hardly made any videos, because I was busy appearing on *Gadget Geeks*. That was great fun. I made whacky stuff like super-fast golf buggies and hi-tech urinals! It also taught me lots of ways to improve my own videos. As fun as working on TV shows is, I still enjoy making my own YouTube videos in The Shed much more.

Super-duper camera

My main camera, which records the best-quality pictures and sound, is a Panasonic AG AC90. This is the camera that's usually fixed to a tripod in The Shed, either up on the bench or on the ground by the doors. It's what I use to do most of the important filming. It's not too big and quite easy to lump around, but I really have to look after it and not bash it about – it cost around £1,000!

Tripods

I have two professional tripods and one cheapie £20 tripod. With a tripod, I can fix the camera in place, and that leaves me free to build or chat in front of it. Most of the time it's just me filming by myself in The Shed, so I need to be able to stick the camera somewhere safe and record what I'm up to. The cheap tripod usually has one of my battered GoPro cameras on it – I use that for filming any stuff that may end up being burnt or exploding!

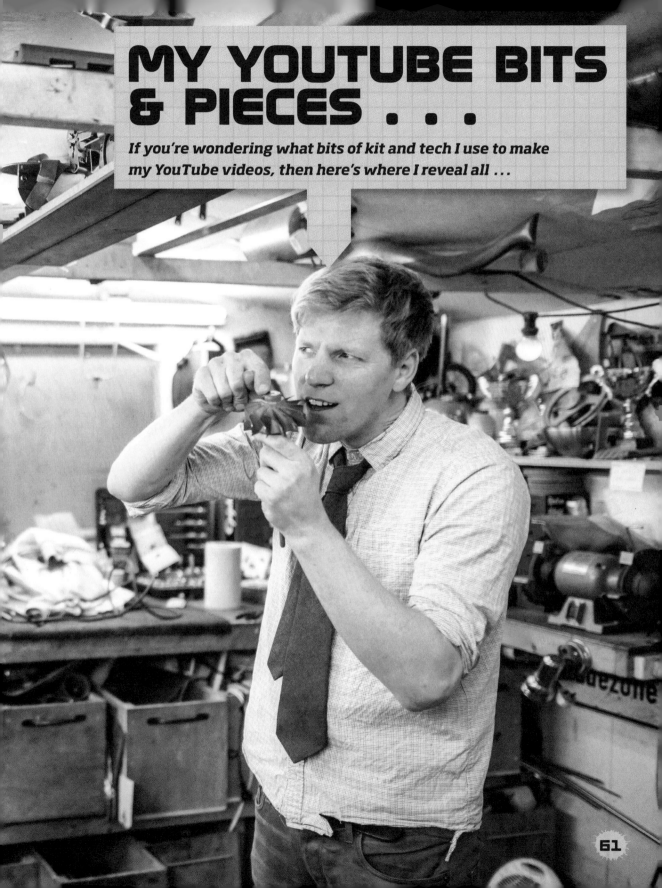

MY YOUTUBE BITS & PIECES . . .

If you're wondering what bits of kit and tech I use to make my YouTube videos, then here's where I reveal all . . .

Gimbal

A gimbal is a clever bit of kit. I can attach a gimbal to the end of a big pole, then stick a GoPro camera on it and record very stable and smooth shots. A gimbal has a self-balancing device, so you can wave the pole and camera around in the air and still get a steady image. A lot of my 360° swing footage was taken from the ground using a gimbal.

GoPro cameras

These are excellent little cameras. They can be stuffed inside machines or strapped to my head, for example, and help to take footage from places that bigger cameras won't fit, or where it's unsafe for me to film! I've used GoPros to get close to fireworks, or attached them to inventions like the fast toilet to record my face. I have two good GoPros that cost about £350 and four cheap ones. The cheap ones usually get smashed around and burnt!

Laptop

Most nights, I spend many hours editing footage on my laptop at my kitchen table. It can take a while to edit all the footage, and that's something that my subscribers obviously don't see – and for good reason, as it can be quite boring! A video of me just editing my YouTube videos would only help to send my viewers to sleep!

Handheld camera

My second camera is smaller, lighter and easier to carry around. This is a Panasonic HDC-SD600, which I bought for about £400. It's perfect for taking selfie-style footage or getting up close to objects . . . or right in Rick's face if I'm feeling really annoying! It can be used on a tripod, but most of the time it's used by me or someone else to capture some action when we're trying out an invention.

How to:
SCREW INTO WOOD

Screwing in screws is another vital part of building the inventions in This Book Isn't Safe! Screws hold pieces of wood, metal or plastic together. This is mega simple to do and also mega effective. Read on, guys and girls . . .

ADULT SUPER VISION NEEDED

1 It doesn't matter what the thickness of the screw is, but a slightly thicker screw will give a bit more strength.

2 To work out the length of the screw you need, first hold the screw against the width of the wood to make sure that when it's screwed in it won't go right through the wood and poke out the other side. You want the screw to go at least halfway into the wood, so that it grabs enough of the wood to hold fast.

3 When screwing into wood, it's a good idea to use a pilot hole to stop the wood from splitting. The depth of your pilot hole needs to be at least three-quarters of the length of the screw going into it. If the wood is quite hard, try to make the pilot hole the same length as the screw.

TOP TIP!
There's an old saying to help you remember which way to turn a screw: 'Righty tighty, Lefty loosey.' If you turn it to the right, the screw will tighten!

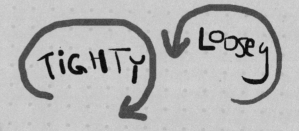

TIGHTY Loosey

4 When you're trying to work out the size of the drill bit to use, first look closely at the size of the main shaft of your screw. The drill bit needs to be roughly the same size as this part of the screw.

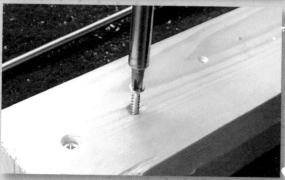

5 Once you've drilled a pilot hole (page 47), you're ready to put a screw in it. Hold the screw upright over the hole with one hand, then put the tip of your screwdriver into the slots on the screw. Slowly turn the screwdriver clockwise and the screw will move into the wood and grip it. If you turn the screw anticlockwise it will come out of the wood.

6 If you're screwing two bits of wood together, clamp them so they won't move. After one screw is in place, you can remove the clamp.

TOP TIP!

Apply constant, gentle, downward pressure to the screwdriver to avoid damaging the head of the screw as you screw it in. The head is the part that your screwdriver connects with. If this is damaged, you'll find it difficult to turn the screw.

Not holding the screwdriver upright is the easiest way to damage a screw!

How to:
TIGHTEN NUTS

Let's go nuts, everyone! Yep, here are the basics of how to tighten nuts, and some notes on why it's important to use nuts, bolts and washers in many of your inventions. Spanners at the ready, please!

1 A bolt is like a screw's cousin. It's pushed through a drilled hole to join two things together. A nut needs to be wound round the end of the bolt that pokes out until the nut clamps down.

2 Only a certain-sized nut will fit properly round a certain-sized bolt. To check you have the right size nut, place the nut over the bolt and ensure that it can be spun round the bolt when you turn it with your fingers, and that it moves down the bolt.

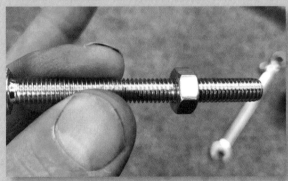

3 Once your bolt is inside the pre-drilled hole, spin the nut down on the end of the bolt. When you've tightened the nut as much as you can with your hand, use a spanner to tighten it a couple of turns more.

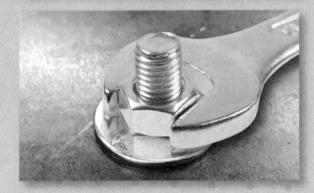

4 It doesn't matter which end of your spanner you use – the open C-shaped end or the ring-spanner end.

TOP TIP!
Don't overtighten the nut, because you could damage the surface of the wood and the nut.

5 Sometimes it's good to use two nuts on top of each other for extra strength. Tighten them both and they'll lock against each other. Hold the first nut still with one spanner while you tighten the other with a second spanner.

6 Adding a simple washer on the bolt before the nut goes on is a good idea. Washers help to protect the surface of the wood by spreading the force of the nut that's applied above it. Washers are very cheap, too.

YOU WILL 'NUT' BELIEVE THIS . . .
I've had this 10mm spanner attached to my key ring since I was fifteen! When I was a teenager, it was handy for fixing my BMX bikes and I've kept it ever since. It's not the best spanner in the world, but has lots of sentimental value.

TOP TIP!
It's best to stick to the same size bolts when you're making an invention. That way you can use the same spanner.

67

FURZE'S PHONE-FILMING THINGY

Back on page 62, I explained how I use a clever gimbal device to attach my camera to a pole and record great shots for my YouTube videos. It's like a steady-cam, and it means the camera can be waved high in the air to capture smooth, swooping images. Brill. Here, I'll show you how to make your own cool gimbal to record amazing videos on a smartphone. It's a mega-neat invention, so I've given it a mega-neat name: Furze's Phone-filming Thingy! Well, no one knows what the word 'gimbal' means, do they?!

'ADULT SUPER VISION NEEDED

'Gimbal' sounds like a monster from the Harry Potter stories!

TOP TIP!

If you have an old wooden-handled broom knocking around, see if you can carefully detach the brush part by unscrewing or sawing it. You can then use the handle to make a Furze's Phone-filming Thingy. Get permission from the broom owner first!*

*I hate it when TV adverts say 'Get permission from the bill payer'! Who is this Bill Payer bloke?!

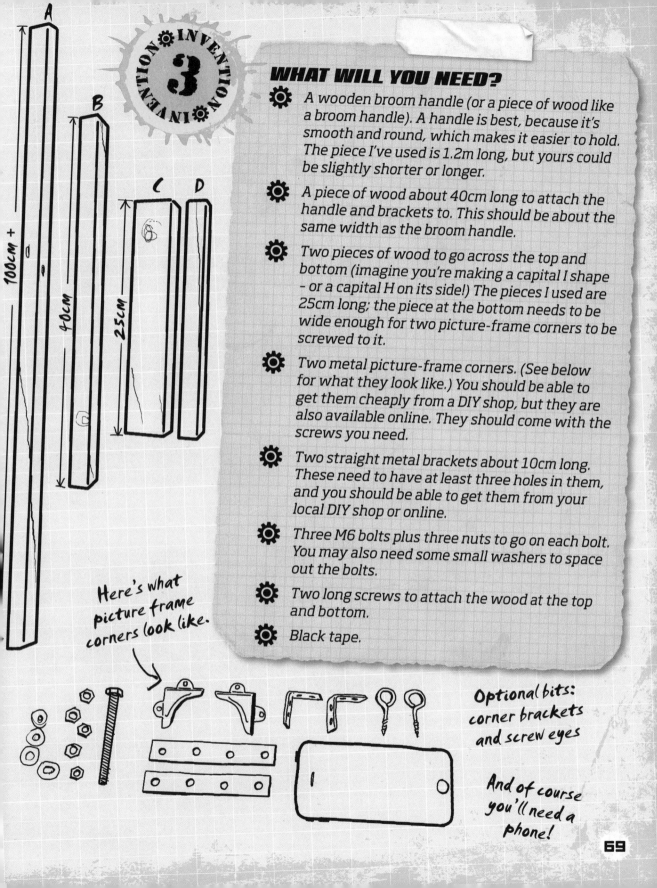

A
100cm +

B
40cm

C D
25cm

WHAT WILL YOU NEED?

⚙ A wooden broom handle (or a piece of wood like a broom handle). A handle is best, because it's smooth and round, which makes it easier to hold. The piece I've used is 1.2m long, but yours could be slightly shorter or longer.

⚙ A piece of wood about 40cm long to attach the handle and brackets to. This should be about the same width as the broom handle.

⚙ Two pieces of wood to go across the top and bottom (imagine you're making a capital I shape – or a capital H on its side!) The pieces I used are 25cm long; the piece at the bottom needs to be wide enough for two picture-frame corners to be screwed to it.

⚙ Two metal picture-frame corners. (See below for what they look like.) You should be able to get them cheaply from a DIY shop, but they are also available online. They should come with the screws you need.

⚙ Two straight metal brackets about 10cm long. These need to have at least three holes in them, and you should be able to get them from your local DIY shop or online.

⚙ Three M6 bolts plus three nuts to go on each bolt. You may also need some small washers to space out the bolts.

⚙ Two long screws to attach the wood at the top and bottom.

⚙ Black tape.

Here's what
picture frame
corners look like.

Optional bits:
corner brackets
and screw eyes

And of course
you'll need a
phone!

STEP 1

Bolt the two metal brackets to piece A of your wood (see diagram on page 69). This is the handle. Put one bracket on the end, making sure two holes are over it. With a pencil, mark a dot through the holes. (My bracket has four holes – the fourth attaches to the long piece of wood and the third isn't used.)

STEP 2

Using a drill bit to match the size of your bolt (in this case 6mm), carefully drill through the two dots, so that the holes go right through. Hold one bracket over the holes, and put a bolt through each. Add the other bracket on the other side, over the ends of the bolts. Tighten a nut on the end of each bolt. Your brackets are now fixed to the handle. Good work!

TOP TIP!

The brackets and the long piece of wood shouldn't touch, otherwise the Furze's Phone-filming Thingy will not pivot properly. If needed, move the brackets apart by adding washers as shown.

STEP 3

Take piece D of your wood and measure and mark where the middle is with a pencil. Drill a pilot hole through the centre of this point, so that you can screw this piece of wood to the top of piece B . Once you've drilled the hole, take a long screw and carefully screw both pieces of wood together.

STEP 4

Attach the bottom piece of wood (piece C – the piece the phone will be attached to) to piece B in the same way. You've now made your capital I or H shape!

TOP TIP!

You can screw little metal L-shaped brackets to the corners of your capital **I** or **H** shape to make it a little stronger, like this

STEP 5

Now it's time to screw the two picture-frame corners to the wood at the bottom. Place your phone in the middle of the wood, then put a bracket on each picture frame corner and mark dots through the holes. Drill pilot holes in each of the four pencil dots, then screw the picture-frame corners to the wood.

Make sure your phone's camera isn't blocked by any of the wood!

TOP TIP!

So that the metal picture-frame corners don't scratch your phone, put a little bit of black tape inside the frame to stop the metal and the phone screen from making contact.

STEP 6

If you've put tape inside the bracket, your phone might no longer fit inside. If so, unscrew the picture-frame screws and place a small washer or nut behind each of the four screws. This raises the corners up a little and lets your phone sit securely.

STEP 7

It's time to attach the handle. About a quarter of the way down from the top of the wood, drill a pilot hole. Line the unbolted ends of the two straight brackets on the handle over the hole and put a bolt through, then gently tighten with a nut on the end.

The Filming Thingy needs to swing freely, so use;
a) a self-locking nut, or
b) a locking washer, or
c) two nuts screwed together

STEP 8

The piece of wood at the bottom needs a counterweight. A counterweight helps make your videos smoother and steadier. I've bolted some large washers on here. Once the counterweight is added, your invention is complete! Whoop whoop!

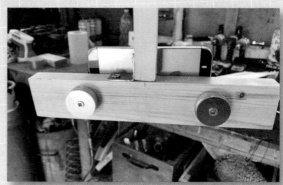

HANG ABOUT . . .

I've also screwed two eye screws (like the ones used for the Brilliant Bedroom-tidy Pulley) into the end of the top piece of wood. If you unscrew and remove the broom handle, you can put a piece of long string through the eye screws then tie it to two points where you want to film. You can then hang Furze's Phone-filming Thingy on the string and slowly move it along to record videos! Pros call this a slide cam.

SWOOP!

COLIN'S CHALLENGE!
How else might you create a simple counterweight? For example, instead of attaching washers, could you simply tie a water bottle to the wood?

••RATING••

STRENGTH:
DETAIL:
DIFFICULTY:

MY YOUTUBE SECRETS

Here are a few tricks, tips and techniques that have helped me become a popular YouTuber over the last ten years ...

TV BIG!

No, this has nothing to do with having a 60-inch widescreen telly. When I appeared on *Gadget Geeks*, the director, Gareth Cornick, along with Laura Offer, taught me valuable lessons. Gareth actually said everything you invent and make must be 'TV big', which means it's gotta look good and flashy and fun on TV. So I like to think that all my inventions have great finishing touches, like the toilet roll and loo brush on the 50-mph toilet, or the lightbulbs and steam on the Christmas Spinner Turkey-cooking Machine.

EDIT AS YOU GO!

I never do all my filming first, then edit the footage. I do a little bit of filming each day in The Shed, then go back into my house and edit what I've shot. That way I can check everything is OK, shoot any little bits again that haven't worked and capture stuff I may have missed. Editing hours and hours of footage in one go doesn't work for me.

WHOOMP

CHOOSE YOUR MUSIC!

Editing a little bit at a time helps me to see what the vibe of the video is, and means I can choose the right type of music to go with it. I often ask my YouTube subscribers to send me their own music, and I've used a lot of rock stuff from the bands Freeze the Atlantic and Heroic. Tip: I'm not going to use boy-band, pop-type tracks, cos I hate it.

TIME IT RIGHT!

My build videos (the ones in which I reveal what I'm making and how to go about building it) are around ten minutes long; subscribers who particularly like these videos want to see quite a lot of what I do in The Shed. The show videos (in which I reveal the invention and how it works) are much shorter at about two or three minutes long. I try to release a new video every one or two weeks to keep my subscribers happy!

Rockin' Rick!

My first YouTube videos used music from my mate Rick and his band, March to the Grave. Cheers, Rickster!

FFSHHWOOOP

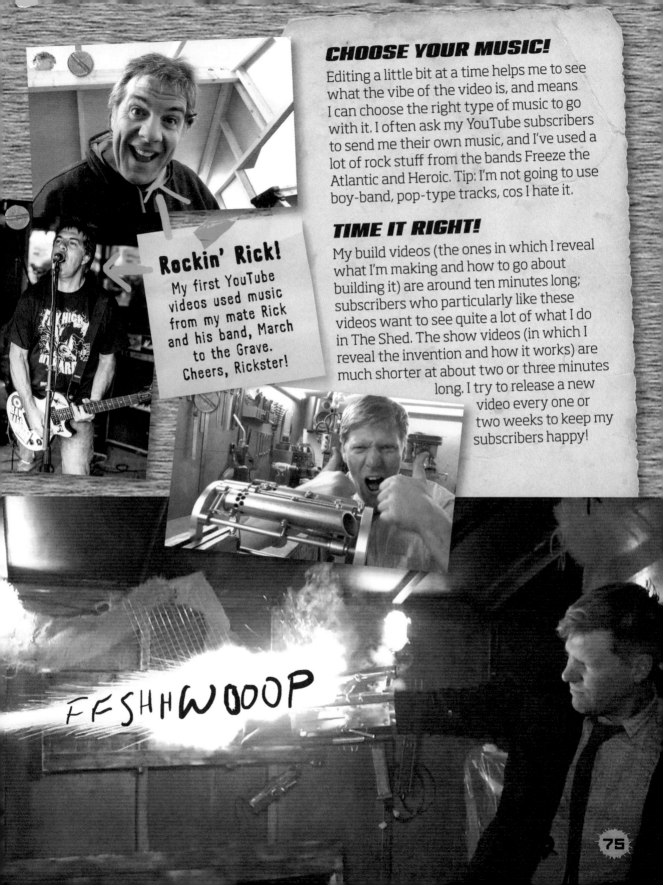

MY YOUTUBE DRESS

Er, I don't mean that I wear a dress in my YouTube videos! I mean how I dress for my YouTube videos. Some people may call me 'that bloke on YouTube who wears a shirt and tie and sets fire to things', and I can't really argue with that. My shirt and tie must be the most famous on the internet!

There's a bit of a story behind my choice of clothing. Many years ago before YouTube, I bought a moped to ride to France and it looked like the moped an old man would ride. So I dressed like one when I rode it, wearing a shirt and tie! Don't question this crazy Furze way, it's just how I roll sometimes. Then, for the Wall of Death video I used the moped and the outfit came with it, of course. I didn't wear a helmet (which I should've done) so the internet named my outfit the 'safety shirt and tie'. It's kind of been my trademark ever since. My thinking was that, if I had the same gear on, people would recognize me and associate me with inventing/building/exploding cool things. A bit like how the TV star Harry Hill always wears the same thing.

I wear two shirts that are pretty much identical. One's long sleeved, and the other is short sleeved – which actually means they're not that identical! My original short-sleeved shirt was unfortunately burned when I had

an accident in The Shed. There was a gas leak on one of my jet engines and it ignited, burning my right arm and making rather a mess of the shirt I had on. I still have the remains of the shirt, though, and one day I'll frame it along with my original grey tie.

You may have seen that I don't wear my famous shirt-and-tie combo when I'm building things. The reason is that they wouldn't last long if I did; they'd get covered in oil and ripped and stained. I wear my shirt and tie when I'm introducing a new video, then when I reveal it and show off the final invention. In the build videos, I usually wear T-shirts and hoodies. Oh, one more thing: I never iron my shirts, as that's a complete waste of time!

A bit of tape keeps my tie out of the way of the drill.

OUCH

77

MAKE YOUR OWN TIE
[just like mine!]

Yes, sir/madam. Here's your chance to create a tie just like mine! Excellent! And here's what you need to do:

Why was the tie really funny?

Cos it was always telling knot-knot jokes!

STEP 1
Take a blank piece of white paper and hold it over the tie at the top of the page.

STEP 2
Trace the outline of the tie with a pen, pencil, felt tip or some lipstick (ask first!).

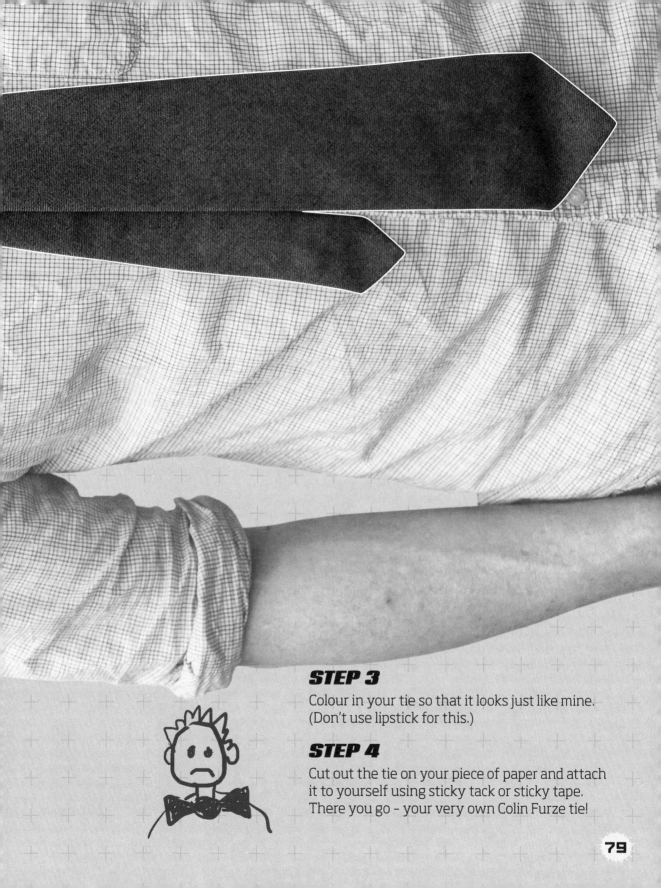

STEP 3

Colour in your tie so that it looks just like mine. (Don't use lipstick for this.)

STEP 4

Cut out the tie on your piece of paper and attach it to yourself using sticky tack or sticky tape. There you go – your very own Colin Furze tie!

IS BEING A YOU

BOOM

SPLAT

NO, IT'S NOT EASY!

I have to mess about in front of the camera every day and spend hours building things and filming. I always need to know exactly what I'm doing, how to do it, and that I have all the materials and tools. Plus it needs to be entertaining for the guys and girls who watch me!

Even YouTubers who just open boxes of toys and things and then talk about them to the camera have to have some talent and knowledge. Try filming yourself talking about random rubbish and see how interesting you are!

I think it's important to stick to what you do best and what your YouTube subscribers expect of you. I turn down all sorts of cool things, like going to movie premieres in the United States and flying fighter jets in the Czech Republic, just because that's not what my channel is about.

My YouTube channel is very popular in Germany. This *may* have something to do with the fact that 'Furze' translates, roughly, to 'fart' in German! I don't think it's easy doing a job where I'm known to an entire nation as **Colin Fart**!

TUBER EASY?!

FZZ

YAY!

YES, IT IS EASY!

OK, I'm not saving lives or helping people like doctors and nurses do, so I guess being a YouTuber is not that vital to the world's existence!

Ignore what I said on the previous page, because YouTubers who JUST OPEN BOXES AND TALK HAVE A REALLY EASY JOB. Well, they do compared to me. I guess I'm just a tad jealous of people who open boxes and still get thousands of views!

When I worked in TV I was made to wear make-up for the cameras and have my hair styled. Ugh! At least being a YouTuber means none of that, so that makes it a much easier job!

THREE OTHER JOBS I'D LOVE TO DO . . .

* Formula One driver!
* Lead guitarist, singer and drummer in a mega rock band!
* Astronaut, cos zero gravity would be epic!

Not sure how I'd do all this at the same time!

MY FAVOURITE INVENTIONS!

The magnet shoes only cos me twenty quid to build. Proper bargain!

The next few pages are stuffed with my crazy creations and mind-boggling machines. Hold on tight, folks!

MAGNET SHOES

These were **cheap**, simple and just made from bits of a microwave, a metal plate and ratchet straps. The end result meant I walked **upside down** on the ceiling of The Shed. That was a world first! I love the magnet shoes cos they're so stupid and **soooo** much fun!

CAKE-O-MATIC

This was a **bonkers** build - a totally and utterly **ridiculous** invention! It was a motor with a rotor on the side that had eight spoons attached to it. When the spoons spun round, I shoved a chocolate cake into it and it **blasted** cake into my gob at lightning speed. Good job I love cake ... but it's a shame I had cake up my nose for weeks afterwards!

I built the Cake-O-Matic on my birthday and used my birthday cake.

PULSE-JET GO-KART

You might have your own go-kart at home, but does it move at a mighty **63mph**? My Pulse-jet Kart does! I invented this because lots of my YouTube subscribers asked me to after I'd made the jet bicycle. It's an old go-kart made bigger, with a whacking-great pulse jet bolted to the back. I could start it by sitting in the seat and fiddling with the gas and levers, which was clever. It **absolutely flew** when I tested it at an airfield!

EEEEEEEEEE

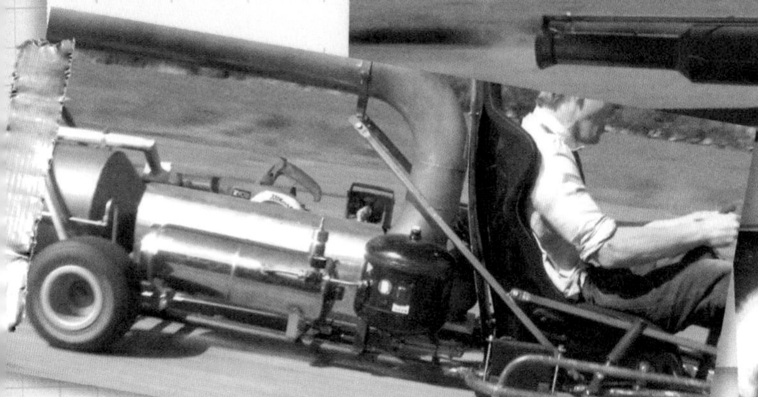

Speedy secret

I may set a world record in the Pulse-jet Kart in the future. I'll need to crack 70mph in it, though!

70

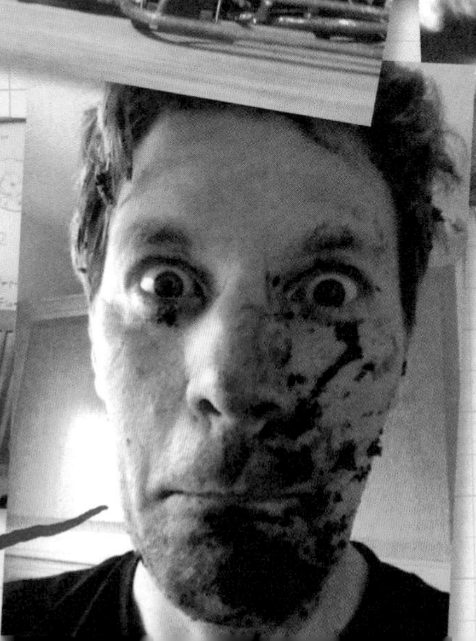

Yum.

hmm...

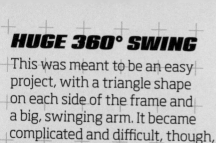

HUGE 360° SWING

This was meant to be an easy project, with a triangle shape on each side of the frame and a big, swinging arm. It became complicated and difficult, though, because it was so huge and so heavy! The axle was 5.5 metres tall and I could see over my house when I swung round. It was great fun and I wasn't scared. Well, maybe just a little bit!

I even strapped on a paramotor like the one I used on the Hoverbike to make the swing go faster. That made me feel sick!

My swing went as high as . . .

* Two female giraffes
* Two double-decker buses
* Fifteen labradoodle dogs

For safety, I first tested the bed in front of a bouncy castle – just in case it shot me into space!

EJECTOR BED

I invented a bed that chucks you out in the morning! It's like the one from the *Wallace & Gromit* films, and I suppose I'm a bit like Wallace. The bed is on a hinged frame, with two pistons underneath that fire up using compression at whatever time you set your alarm for. You'll never be late for school again!

AARGH!

FHHWiiiT!

WOLVERINE'S CLAWS

Wolverine is a cool character from the X-Men comics and movies. I recreated his famous 'Adamantium' claws, which shoot out from his fists. This was the first time I had copied something that already existed, and it was awesome and worked really well. I felt like a true superhero, and these videos really got me noticed on YouTube. **Fhhhwiiit!**

That's the noise the claws make coming out, not the sound of me farting!

TOASTER KNIFE

I usually invent things that no company would ever make, because my stuff (and my brain!) is just too crazy. But the Toaster Knife is about as close as I've come to making something that might be sold in a shop. It uses a modified transformer from a microwave connected to electrical cables to heat a knife until it gets incredibly hot. This knife cuts AND toasts bread at the same time. It's one of my fave inventions!

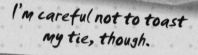

I like to use my Toaster Knife in the dark, cos then I can see the blade glow red hot.

I'm careful not to toast my tie, though.

BRAPP BRAPP BRRAH

WOOF

VSSSH

VSSSH

HOVERBIKE

Wow! This was a barking-mad idea. I always thought that, if I had a couple of big fan motors that kicked out 60-70kg of thrust each, that should be able to lift me (weighing 80kg) off the ground. The Hoverbike worked, but it was a nightmare to steer and fly. I don't think we'll all zoom around on Hoverbikes in the future, cos they're very tricky to navigate!

PULSE-JET BICYCLE

This invention is one of my most popular YouTube videos. It's completely nutty! I took an old Raleigh shopper bike, made it longer and welded a massive metal pulse jet to it. This uses gas, air and loads of flames to propel the bike to a ridiculous **50mph**. The only problem was I kept getting punctures!

Er, that was my mum's bike I destroyed. I hope she doesn't want it back!

MEGA MILK-BOTTLE RAFT

When I was about ten, I made lots of little rafts with my mates out of wooden pallets and plastic barrels tied together with rope. It was awesome fun messing about with them in shallow and safe water - and they hardly ever sank, which was a bonus! I'm going to take you through building your own simple raft, and give you the chance to float on water, just like I did.

WHAT WILL YOU NEED?

⚙ Lots of empty plastic milk bottles with handles! See the Sciencey Bit opposite to work out the exact number you'll need.

⚙ Several pieces of wood. Turn over the page and read the steps to see how much you may need.

⚙ Plenty of wood screws, probably around 30 and some cord.

⚙ A pair of wellies.* (This is actually for when you take the raft on to the water after you've built it.)

*TOP TIP!
Don't use your Concrete-crusher Wellies, cos they're not very waterproof!

HMS MOO

BUOYORP!

Mi

Milk

TOP TIP!

If you can, use the same style of empty plastic milk bottle from the same shop or supermarket. This means the shape and size of the handles will be the same on all of them. And don't use ones with the handle on the corner, like this:

SCIENCEY BIT

You'll be using empty plastic milk bottles as your raft's buoyancy aid (the bit that keeps you on top of the water). The average plastic milk bottle in Britain is just over 2 litres in size. And 1 litre of air displaces 1kg of water.

To work out how many bottles you will need, follow this easy formula (and get a grown-up to double-check it for you):
Your weight in kg ÷ 2 = Number of milk bottles you'll need
So, if you weigh 30kg, it will look like this:
30 ÷ 2 = 15 milk bottles
Remember to round up, not down, to be on the safe side.

Phew, that's the science bit over!

STEP 1

You need to make two rows of an equal number of empty plastic milk bottles – so, if you're using twenty bottles, make two rows of ten. (See page 89 to work out how many you need.) Lay the rows of bottles on the ground, handles facing up.

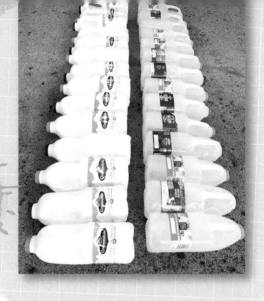

STEP 2

You need pieces of wood long enough to slot through the bottle handles in each row. If you have a wooden pallet, you could take it apart and use the wood, or use two long pieces of wood from a DIY shop. Thread one piece of wood through the handles of each row.

TOP TIP!

If the wood is slightly too thick to slide through the handles, you can sand the edges off it using sandpaper. If you don't have any sandpaper, you can get it quite cheaply from DIY shops. To sand the edges, just rub the sandpaper (sanded side down) back and forth along the edges of the wood.

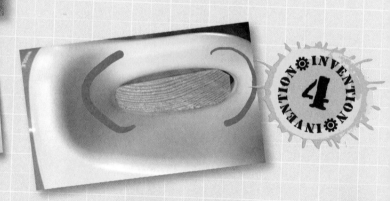

STEP 3

Place your two rows of empty plastic milk bottles (with the wood still threaded through the handles) firmly beside each other. Now measure the **width** of these rows. Saw two pieces of wood to the same length as this width.

STEP 4

Measure the LENGTH of the top of your raft, as shown. You will need three or five pieces of wood this length depending on the width of your wood. (See pictures in Step 7 below.)

STEP 5

Lay out two of your long pieces of wood and the two short pieces in a neat rectangle, as shown. Mark and drill two pilot holes in each corner, where the wood overlaps. Don't make the holes too near the ends. Countersink the holes for a neater finish.

STEP 6

Screw the four pieces together at each corner. This is the top of your raft. Check there are no sharp bits anywhere – this is the part you'll sit on in the water! Next, measure and mark the middle of the end pieces.

STEP 7

Fix a third long piece of wood to the middle of the rectangle, lining up to the centre marks you made. Then (if you need them) fix two more long pieces in between, as shown. Always drill pilot holes and countersink them. The raft top – or deck – is finished. Yay!

STEP 8

Rest the deck on top of the milk bottles. The two long pieces of wood (pushed through the bottle handles) will stick out at each end. Mark where the deck ends on these pieces, and cut off the spare wood.

STEP 9

Turn the deck upside down. Place the bottles on top of the deck and screw them to the underneath of the deck in each corner. Pilot holes! Countersink! I don't need to tell you that again, do I?

STEP 10

Are you done? Almost. Screw a big screw eye to the middle at one end of your raft. Firmly tie a good strong bit of cord to the screw eye. Then give your raft a name!

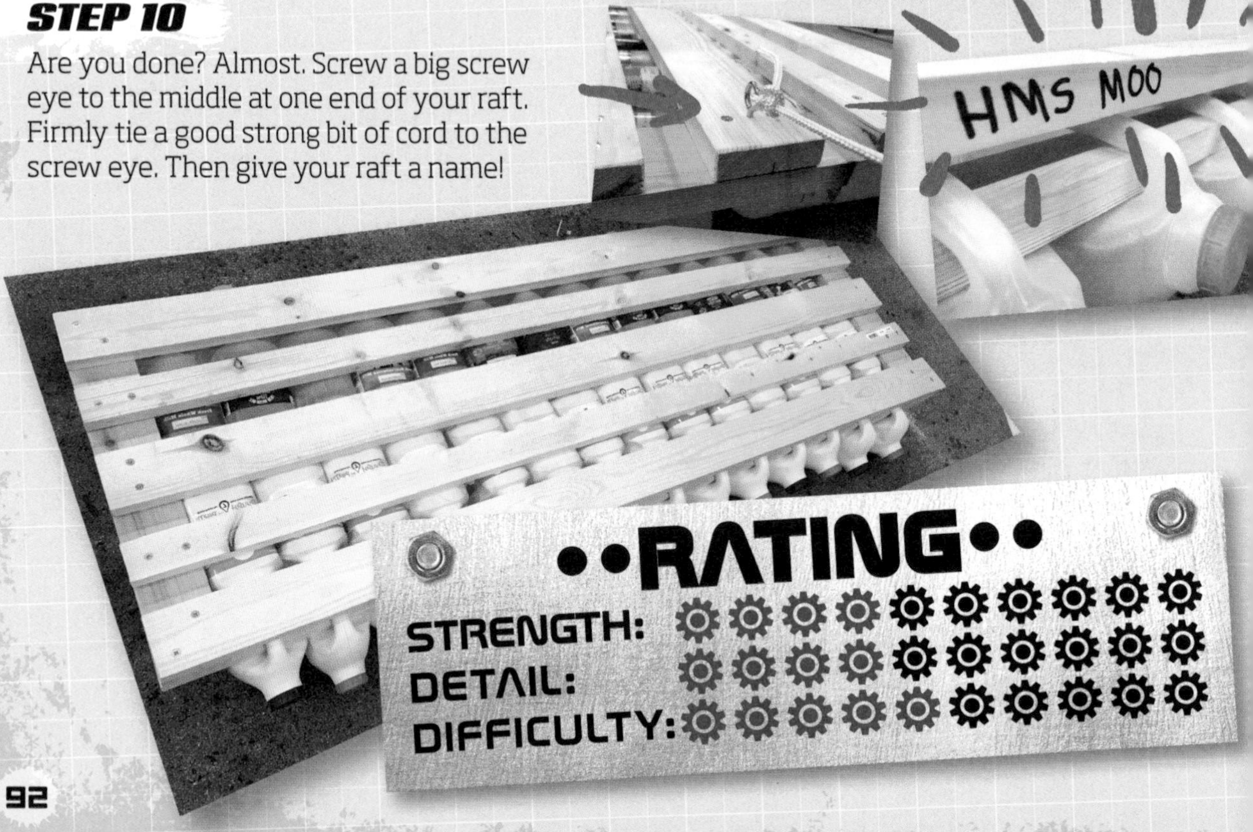

HMS MOO

••RATING••

STRENGTH:
DETAIL:
DIFFICULTY:

COLIN'S CHALLENGE
If you're confident with your wood-cutting and measuring skills, you could make a pointy boat-like end on your raft as in the picture to the right.

WHY NOT?
Why not build a little wooden flagpole to attach to your raft? You could also paint the milk bottles to make your invention look even cooler!

TOP TIP!
To test how deep the water is, find a long stick or piece of wood. Then, from a safe place beside the water, carefully poke the stick into the water. If you can feel the bottom of the river or lake with the stick, and it's not deeper than your waist, then it could be a good spot to test your raft.

ADULT SUPERVISION!
You MUST, MUST, MUST have adult supervision whenever you take your raft out on to water. Don't take it in water that's deeper than your waist and stick to clean, quiet, shallow ponds and lakes.

MY AWESOME SHED!

The Queen has Buckingham Palace, the Doctor has the TARDIS and, er, Batman has the Batcave. The place I like to call home is The Shed. Great name, that.

DANGER
5000 VOLTS
DO NOT ENTER
WITHOUT PERMISSION
OF THE CHIEF ENGINEER

If you want to build, create and invent things, then it's ideal to have your own space, a safe place to saw, screw and stick stuff, where it doesn't matter if you make a mess. Try to keep it a bit tidy, though, so you don't waste time looking for tools like, say, your 12-mm spanner.*

I wasn't allowed in my dad's shed when I was a lad, which was a big shame. When my dad passed away in 2007, I could finally get into his shed to use the benches and tools, and have the space to be creative. Then in 2009 I bought a house with my girlfriend and I finally got the chance to have my *own* shed. Hurrah! I built The Shed myself. I laid the concrete foundation in nice autumn weather, but then I had to leave it for a few months because I was busy being a plumber during the day. It was January when I finally began to build the wooden frame of the shed (it was flippin' freezing!) and it took about a month to finish. The Shed is fully insulated and has proper electrics, loads of space for my tools and gear, and big benches. I really love The Shed. Love it, love it, love it!

*I know exactly where my 12-mm spanner is - it's between my 10-mm spanner and my 13-mm spanner!

The first thing I built in The Shed was my flame-throwing scooter, which actually got me into a little trouble with the police. Whoops.

INSIDE MY AWESOME SHED!

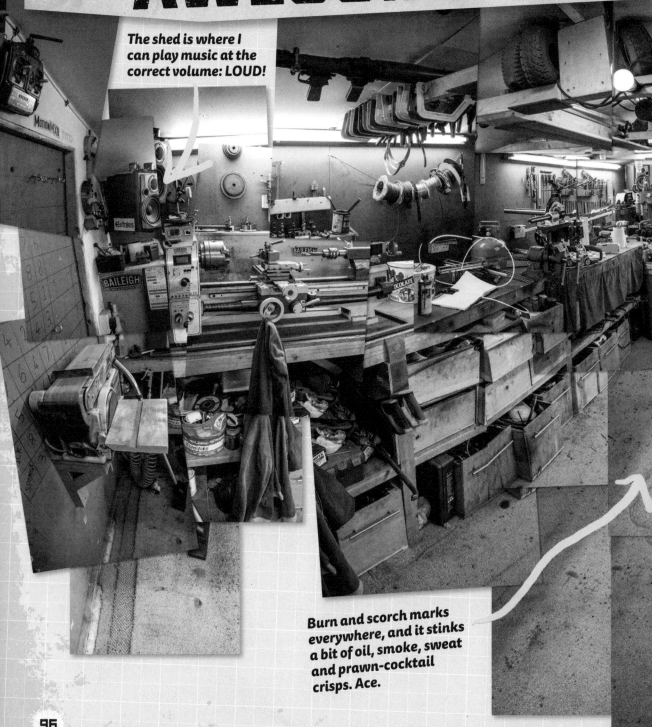

The shed is where I can play music at the correct volume: LOUD!

Burn and scorch marks everywhere, and it stinks a bit of oil, smoke, sweat and prawn-cocktail crisps. Ace.

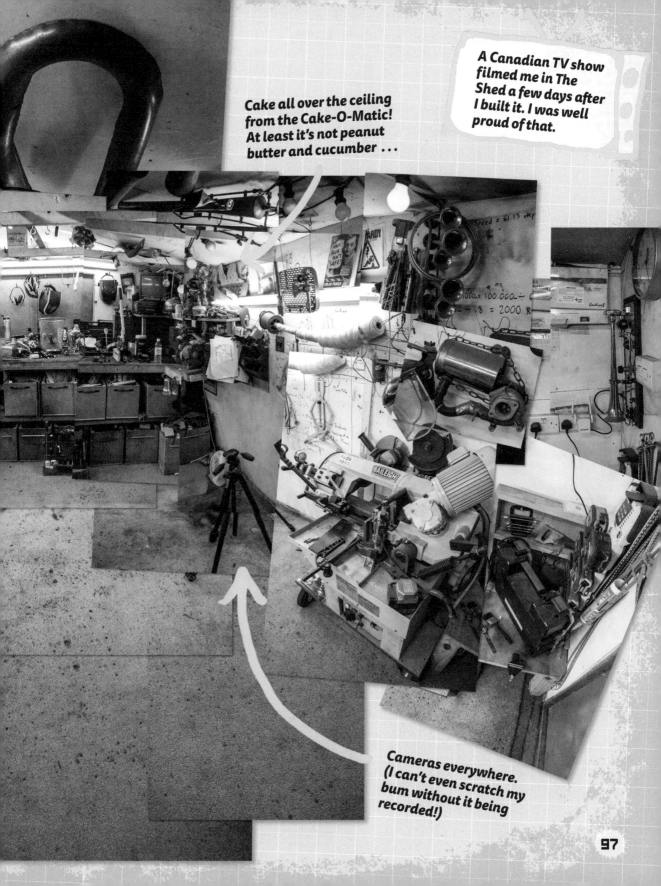

Cake all over the ceiling from the Cake-O-Matic! At least it's not peanut butter and cucumber . . .

A Canadian TV show filmed me in The Shed a few days after I built it. I was well proud of that.

Cameras everywhere. (I can't even scratch my bum without it being recorded!)

MY OTHER AWESOME SHED!

Why have one shed when you can have two? My other shed in the garden is called The Bunker Shed, because, well, it goes over the hatch entrance to my underground bunker. Mega cool, hey?!

I used to have an old 1970s shed where this one is now, but I took it down to make room for the bunker. Instead of spending about £1,600 on a new shed from a garden centre, which would have been flimsy and a bit rubbish, I spent the cash on buying the materials for and building my own second shed, which is super strong and looks much better. It's exactly the same design as The Shed, so I guess I could've called it The Shed's Little Brother Shed, but that would just be ridiculous. It's also fully insulated and has a rather fancy slate roof. Inside are things like the lawn mower, a bouncy castle, some of my inventions, and other bits and pieces. So I've gone from dreaming of one day having my own shed to having two awesome sheds to muck about in. Happy days!

Will I eventually have a third shed? Never say never, but I do also have a wooden castle that I built for my kids in a day out of wooden pallets. That'll do for now.

Veggie shed!

The smaller shed that The Bunker Shed replaced is now on my mum's allotment, surrounded by cabbages and green beans. I'm pretty sure it's much quieter there than in my garden!

SEVEN SHED SECRETS!

Shed Seven is the name of a music band from the 1990s, so I thought it'd be funny to say 'seven shed secrets'. Ha, ha! Huh, you're not laughing? Never mind...

It's time to discover some cool secrets about my special sheds. After all, my sheds feature in everything I make and most of my YouTube videos. If there's no shed, there's no Colin Furze, I reckon!

1 The Shed has **three** carpets. People always ask why it's carpeted, especially when it gets covered in petrol, grease, gunk, tea and baked beans. Having carpet means I don't get cold feet in the winter. Smart idea.

Whoops, got a bit melty

2 **The Stig** has been in The Shed. Yep, the super-speedy racing driver from the *Top Gear* TV show was delivered to The Shed in a box before he tested the mega-quick dodgem car I created. The Stig didn't say much. Actually, he said zilch all day.

3 When I made the Thermite Launcher, which is a crazy handheld machine that spits balls of fire, I was filming the YouTube video in The Shed until **3 a.m.!** I don't know how I stayed awa-...zzzz...snore...zzzzzzz...

4 The Shed used to be an **igloo**. Kind of. I made the concrete floor base first, and then it snowed, so I made an igloo on the floor and built The Shed's wooden frame around it. The igloo eventually melted. Sad times.

5 My young son, **Jake**, helped me build The Bunker Shed. He also has his own little workbench in the corner of The Shed. Good work, son!

6 TV presenter **Steve Jones** bangs his head in The Shed! He's the Welsh guy who presents *Formula One* on Channel 4, and when we filmed something once, he kept knocking his bonce on the roof. Steve's quite tall.

7 I'm going to build a **winch** at the top of the hatch on The Bunker Shed. Then I'll be able to get things up and down easily and won't have to drag stuff while I climb the ladder.

101

MY ULTIMATE UNDER-GROUND BUNKER!

Thermite Launcher

Ejector Bed

Doorbell

Heated slipper

HIGH VOLTAGE

This is one of the coolest things I've ever done. Maybe even one of the best things a human has ever done? Basically, Sky had a new drama called You, Me and the Apocalypse *and the TV bosses asked me what I would do if the world was about to end. I said I'd build an underground bunker in my garden to escape to . . . and they told me to do just that! Brrrriiillllliiiaannnnttttt!*

Ladder to surface

Duvet to keep the heat and noise in

Turkey Spinner

Spare paramotor

Star Wars Stormtrooper helmet

Emergency food supplies

FAB
FRISBEE
FLINGER

One thing that's not best suited to being used in the underground bunker is my Fab Frisbee Flinger. This is another ultra-cool invention I'm about to show you how to build, but it needs plenty of outdoor space!

YOU WILL NEED

- ⚙ Various lengths of wood – about 3.5m in total. It's probably best to use the same sort of wood throughout, so that it fits together well and looks neat. I've used different lengths of wood about 70-mm wide and 40-mm thick, but there's no need for the wood you use to be the same width and thickness as mine. All the wood you use needs to be fairly sturdy and chunky to give this invention some strength.

- ⚙ Two cardboard strips about 50–60cm long and 15–20 cm wide.

- ⚙ A 10-cm-long threaded bolt. This should be easy to get hold of from a DIY or hardware store.

- ⚙ Four nuts and washers that will fit the bolt.

- ⚙ Some screws.

- ⚙ Two screw eyes, like the ones used on the Brilliant Bedroom-tidy Pulley.

- ⚙ Between two and six bungee cords. They vary in length and any size will work. Lots of people use them to secure luggage in the car, stuff to the garage wall and so on. DIY shops sell them, but you can usually get a load really cheap from a pound shop.

- ⚙ Strong tape.

- ⚙ A Frisbee, of course!*

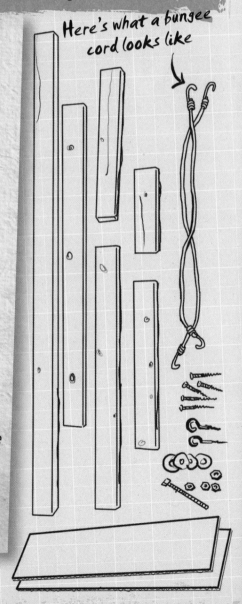

Here's what a bungee cord looks like

* Don't try flinging your parents' favourite dinner plates. I don't think they'd be too chuffed.

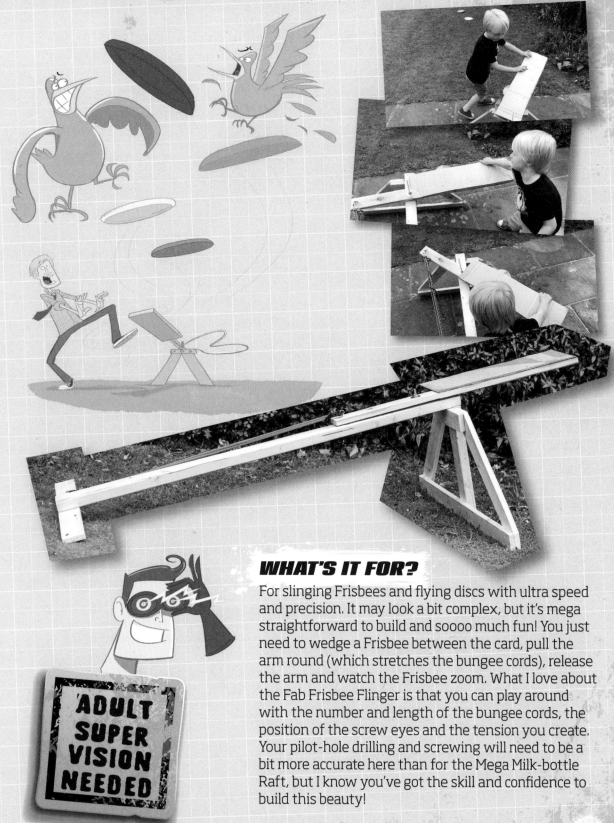

WHAT'S IT FOR?

For slinging Frisbees and flying discs with ultra speed and precision. It may look a bit complex, but it's mega straightforward to build and soooo much fun! You just need to wedge a Frisbee between the card, pull the arm round (which stretches the bungee cords), release the arm and watch the Frisbee zoom. What I love about the Fab Frisbee Flinger is that you can play around with the number and length of the bungee cords, the position of the screw eyes and the tension you create. Your pilot-hole drilling and screwing will need to be a bit more accurate here than for the Mega Milk-bottle Raft, but I know you've got the skill and confidence to build this beauty!

ADULT
SUPER
VISION
NEEDED

STEP 1

Let's start with your longest piece of wood – this bit will make the main cross of your Fab Frisbee Flinger. The piece I've used is 1.5m long, but your piece could be slightly longer or shorter.

STEP 2

Next you'll need to attach a piece of wood to the bottom of this long bit, so that it runs horizontally at the base. (I used a 50-cm-long piece.) Measure where the middle of the wood is and mark it with a pencil. Drill a pilot hole through the smaller piece into the larger one, then screw the two bits of wood together. You might want to make two holes and use two screws, depending on the size and weight of your wood.

STEP 3

The next stage is to attach a vertical bit of wood at the end opposite the piece you've already screwed on. This third piece will lift the invention up so that the long piece in the middle will be at an angle. The piece I used is 45cm long, but yours doesn't have to be the same. Drill a pilot hole through the end of your long bit of wood and into your third piece. Screw these bits of wood together.

STEP 4

More wood screwing! (There's a lot of wood in this invention!) You need to attach a horizontal piece of wood to the end of the bit you fixed on in Step 3. (The piece I used here is 80cm.) Measure the middle of your piece of wood, and line this up with the middle of the vertical piece. Drill a pilot hole and screw the two together.

STEP 5

The Fab Frisbee Flinger now needs a small piece of wood behind the vertical wood that you fixed in Step 3, ensuring that it's touching the long bit. The piece I used is 25cm long. Mark the middle of the wood, drill a pilot hole and screw the two together.

STEP 6

Now you just need to add two pieces that go at an angle on either side at the front. (Refer to the picture in Step 8 to see what you're aiming to achieve.) You actually want the pieces of wood to be slightly longer and overlap with the pieces from Steps 4 and 5 in order to be able to cut them off neatly in Step 7.

STEP 7

Draw a line across both ends of one piece of the wood from Step 6, in line with the pieces you added in Steps 4 and 5. Carefully saw along your lines. Line the pieces of wood up and screw them together.

STEP 8

Repeat Step 7 with the other piece of angled wood. You've now made all the wooden parts and you just need to construct the arm. Congrats to you!

STEP 9

The length of wood I used for my flinger arm is 1m and needs to be thicker than the Frisbee. Mark a dot on the wide edge of the wood you're going to use for your Flinger arm one-third of the way from the bottom – about 33cm for my piece of wood. Drill a hole wide enough to take your bolt through the wood at this dot.

STEP 10

Now measure and mark a dot 30cm from the raised end of the very longest piece of wood on the flinger. Drill a hole wide enough to take your bolt through the wood at this dot, too.

STEP 11

Thread a washer on the bolt, and push the bolt up through the hole in the flinger frame. Add a second washer to the bolt and screw on a nut. Finally, drop on a third washer.

STEP 12

Slide the flinger arm over the bolt, add a final washer and then screw on two nuts. Don't tighten the bottom one too much – the flinger arm has to move easily. Hold the bottom nut in place with one spanner while you tighten the top one with another spanner.

STEP 13

Now you need to attach the screw eyes, which hold the bungee cords. Drill a pilot hole about 5cm from the bottom of the longest piece of wood, then screw in a screw eye.

STEP 14

My fave number, remember?!

At the bottom of the flinger arm, about 5cm from the edge, drill another pilot hole and attach the other screw eye. You can now hook on your bungee cords, or wrap them round the hooks.

STEP 15

Finally, the cardboard needs to be added to each side of the flinger arm. Measure from the top of the arm down to about 5cm from where the bolt pivot is. This is the length of card you'll need on each side. Cut two pieces of cardboard and attach them with strong tape or small screws.

STEP 16

Your Fab Frisbee Flinger is finished! Wedge a Frisbee into the card, pull the top of the flinger arm round to the bottom, then stand back and release the arm. Your Frisbee should fly like a rocket off into the distance!

wheee!!

••RATING••

STRENGTH: ⚙⚙⚙⚙⚙⚙⚙⚙⚙⚙
DETAIL: ⚙⚙⚙⚙⚙⚙⚙⚙⚙⚙
DIFFICULTY: ⚙⚙⚙⚙⚙⚙⚙⚙⚙⚙

TOP TIP!

Make sure no one is in front of the Fab Frisbee Flinger or anywhere they could get hit. If anyone is watching, they should stand behind the invention too, just in case the Frisbee shoots off at a weird angle!

HALF-TIME BREAK

Yes indeedy-deedy! You've reached the halfway point of This Book Isn't Safe! and so far you've learned how to build five of the ten fantastic inventions.

Actually, this isn't the exact halfway point, because this is page 110 and my book is 192 pages; the exact halfway mark was back on page 96, but at that point I was banging on about how amazing The Shed is and it didn't feel like the right moment for a half-time break. Soz, I'm totally waffling . . . but now is the perfect place for a half-time break!

If you've made the five inventions so far, you've discovered how to . . .

- ✸ *Mix concrete*
- ✸ *Use a screwdriver and tighten screws*
- ✸ *Tighten bolts with nuts and washers*
- ✸ *Saw wood*
- ✸ *Drill into wood*
- ✸ *Countersink a screw*
- ✸ *Measure accurately*
- ✸ *Use a screw eye*
- ✸ *Apply force using bungee cords*

That's actually quite a lot of new things you've discovered, and throughout the rest of the book you'll be DOING EVEN MORE MEGA THINGS! So, half-time break's over, people. Put your pencil back behind your ear, turn the page and carry on learning lots about how to make whacky inventions.

ZZZZZ

BOURBON

COLIN'S TEA

Yes I have my own tea.
One of the perks of fame!

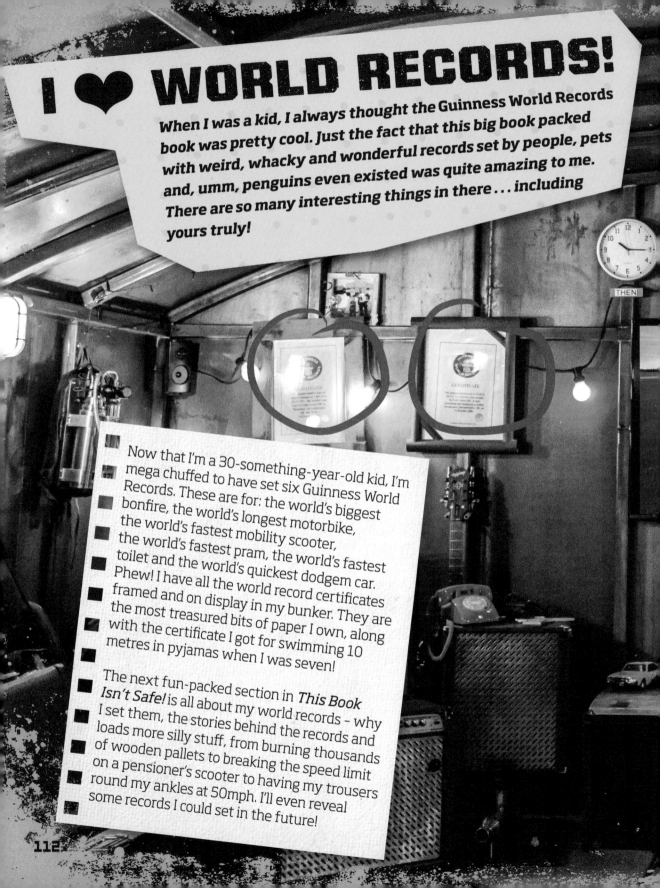

I ♥ WORLD RECORDS!

When I was a kid, I always thought the Guinness World Records book was pretty cool. Just the fact that this big book packed with weird, whacky and wonderful records set by people, pets and, umm, penguins even existed was quite amazing to me. There are so many interesting things in there . . . including yours truly!

Now that I'm a 30-something-year-old kid, I'm mega chuffed to have set six Guinness World Records. These are for: the world's biggest bonfire, the world's longest motorbike, the world's fastest mobility scooter, the world's fastest pram, the world's fastest toilet and the world's quickest dodgem car. Phew! I have all the world record certificates framed and on display in my bunker. They are the most treasured bits of paper I own, along with the certificate I got for swimming 10 metres in pyjamas when I was seven!

The next fun-packed section in *This Book Isn't Safe!* is all about my world records – why I set them, the stories behind the records and loads more silly stuff, from burning thousands of wooden pallets to breaking the speed limit on a pensioner's scooter to having my trousers round my ankles at 50mph. I'll even reveal some records I could set in the future!

CRAZIEST WORLD RECORDS!

I didn't set these records, but they're totally bonkers:

⚙ The world's largest cup of tea held 4,000 litres and was 3 metres tall!

⚙ A man held 496 drinking straws in his mouth - he even had his teeth removed to fit more in! Eurgh!

⚙ Somehow, 29 people crammed into a Mini car in China. Did some hide in the glovebox?!

1,401.6 CUBIC METRES OF FIRE

(the world's biggest bonfire, in other words!)

Claiming the record for the world's biggest bonfire is what started my quest to be a multiple world-record holder. I like fire, I like big things and I like doing unusual stuff - the bonfire ticked all three boxes! I was looking at the Guinness World Records website one day and thought, This could be a cool thing to do ... Well, a hot thing, actually! It took me well over a year to get ready to set the record, though.

I built my bonfire using wooden pallets. A pallet is a flat structure that supermarkets, warehouses and industrial companies use to store products on – items are stacked on top of a pallet and a forklift truck usually loads the pallets on and off a lorry. I needed quite a few pallets to build the bonfire ... about **24,000** of them!

BIG BONFIRE FACTS . . .

* I bought my beloved old Toyota Hilux pick-up truck just to move the bonfire pallets to the field.

* The bonfire video was my first YouTube hit. YouTube started to become very popular around the same time.

* I used 850 leftover pallets to build the circular Wall of Death for my motorbike video soon after.

That was a monster amount of pallets – and I was going to arrange them in a pyramid then set fire to them in the middle of a farmer's field in Rutland! But, a few weeks before the bonfire was to be lit, the farmer discovered that I was arranging the pallets on top of a high-pressure gas main. Whoops! So, the day before the world record, I had to move the pallets to another (safer) field . . . and they ended up being arranged in a big, pointy rectangle-type shape.

With the help of a few hundred onlookers, I lit the fire on my birthday in 2006 and captured the record. I was very, very, very pleased. And I very, very, very much stank of burnt wood and smoke for the next six weeks!

MY MEGA

World record numero two-o was just the small matter of me making the world's longest motorbike. Look at it - the thing is 14 metres long!

loong!

2ⁿᵈ WORLD RECORD

Again, this is a totally stupid record and this bike is one of the most impractical machines ever to be given two wheels. The ludicrously long bike *did* work, but it was tough to steer and a nightmare going round corners.

The original motorbike is actually the one I used for the Wall of Death motorbike trick. I sort of chopped it in half, with the handlebars and one wheel at the front and the engine, exhaust and rear wheel all the way down at the back. Between the front and the back were metres and metres of metal tubing – the whole thing looked like scaffolding on wheels! Amazingly, it stayed together and I took it to 30mph on an airfield – it'd be illegal for me to ride it on public roads.

I got my world record certificate about six weeks later, so it was worth all the hassle. It was actually the easiest record I've achieved . . . but I've had to take the motorbike apart, as it took up so much room in my garden!

MOTORBIKE!

It's . . .
* as long as 7.9 Colin Furzes!
* as wide as two full-size footy goals!
* longer than the average limousine!

I needed the trusty Toyota to take it anywhere!

This bike's even loooooonger!

After this world record, a company that sells bikes challenged me to make an even longer motorbike! Of course I did just that - it was **22 metres**!

looonger!

SUPER-SPEEDY

Mobility scooters are wonderful things for those who can't get around very easily. They are sensible and practical.

But I'm not a very sensible or practical person. So in 2010, I wondered if I could set a Guinness World Record for building the fastest mobility scooter. Here are a few facts to consider . . .

- *A mobility scooter has a top speed of 4mph.*
- *Mobility scooters have simple electric motors.*
- *The basket at the front carries the shopping.*

Now, my mobility scooter was a little bit different . . .

- *I built my scooter for speeds over 70mph.*
- *It had a 125cc motorbike engine.*
- *The basket at the front carried the fuel tank (no room for the shopping).*

Pretty cool, hey? I started with a standard Pride Legend scooter and stripped out the motor. I made the chassis longer, bolted in the engine, strapped a totally bonkers Formula One-style exhaust to the back, and the whole thing looked like a, well, it looked like a mobility scooter! That was the point, though – I wanted my scooter to look just like a normal scooter.

wheeee!

SCOOTER!

3rd WORLD RECORD

wheelie

Except it wasn't normal at all. I recorded a mind-boggling speed of **71.59mph** (breaking the UK's speed limit!) and bagged world record number three in the process. Marvellous. Just don't let your grandpa ever ride it, cos he'll spill his shopping all over the pavement.

VIV

I call the mobility scooter VIV. Not Viv as in 'Vivian' but as in '**V**ery **I**mportant **V**ideo'. The scooter video gave my YouTube channel a big boost. I appeared on *Russell Howard's Good News* to talk about it, which led to the *Gadget Geeks* stuff, which led to me not being a plumber and becoming a full-time YouTuber. All thanks to my super-speedy scooter!

THE MEGA-QUICK MEGAPRAM!

In 2012, I had a monumental brainwave. My lovely girlfriend, Charlotte, was about to have our first child. We'd been to the shops to buy a pram for the little 'un, but looking at all the prams left me thinking, Where are the cool prams?!

4th WORLD RECORD

WHEELY FUNNY!
The Megapram had wheels from a skateboard at first, but I went so fast that they melted!

Stainless-steel buggy

Four gears with Formula One-style button shifters

125cc motorbike engine with ten-brake horsepower

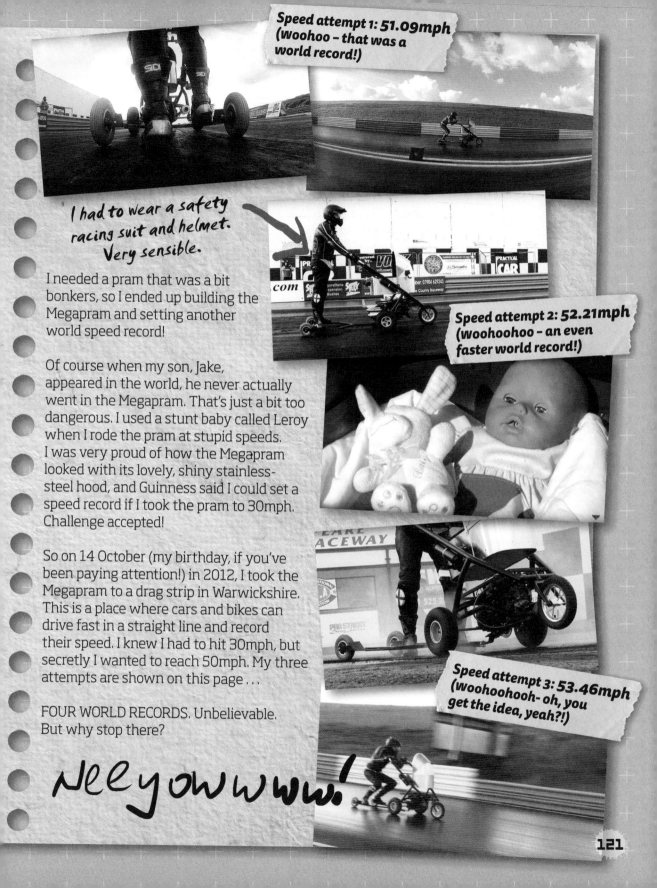

I had to wear a safety racing suit and helmet. Very sensible.

I needed a pram that was a bit bonkers, so I ended up building the Megapram and setting another world speed record!

Of course when my son, Jake, appeared in the world, he never actually went in the Megapram. That's just a bit too dangerous. I used a stunt baby called Leroy when I rode the pram at stupid speeds. I was very proud of how the Megapram looked with its lovely, shiny stainless-steel hood, and Guinness said I could set a speed record if I took the pram to 30mph. Challenge accepted!

So on 14 October (my birthday, if you've been paying attention!) in 2012, I took the Megapram to a drag strip in Warwickshire. This is a place where cars and bikes can drive fast in a straight line and record their speed. I knew I had to hit 30mph, but secretly I wanted to reach 50mph. My three attempts are shown on this page . . .

FOUR WORLD RECORDS. Unbelievable. But why stop there?

Neeyowwww!

Speed attempt 2: 52.21mph (woohoohoo – an even faster world record!)

Speed attempt 3: 53.46mph (woohoohooh- oh, you get the idea, yeah?!)

121

cover your eyes ... PANTS ALERT!

The record that lots of people know me for is when I built the world's fastest toilet. This means that millions have seen me on YouTube, sitting on a toilet with my pants on display and my trousers round my ankles. How awkward is that?!

People laugh at it, but it was also great fun to do and it took me back to my plumbing days when I used to fit and fix toilets all the time. The speed record that I needed to break was 42.25mph, set by a chap called Ed China in Italy in 2011. I was confident I could break that record, but I wanted to do it on a machine that also looked like a real loo, and not just a toilet strapped to a go-kart.

I used the chassis from a mobility scooter (again) and made it bigger and added a motorbike engine. This had a wooden box bolted to it so the toilet could sit on the top. My toilet had gears, which were operated by the loo brush, and loads of other exciting extras. I had to take the toilet to a drag strip to try to set the world record. Did I succeed? Take a look at the next page to find out ... or, if you can't wait that long, just rearrange these words to reveal the answer:

I RECORD DID SET YES TOILET A SPEED WORLD SITTING ON A.

TOILET TEST!

Since I used to be a plumber, I know loads about toilets. Tick your answers to my crazy questions.

1 What's the bendy bit at the bottom of a toilet called?
- ☐ U-bend
- ☐ Steve
- ☐ YouTube-bend

2 Which of the following are toilets usually made from?
- ☐ potatoes
- ☐ polyester
- ☐ porcelain

3 What do you usually find next to a toilet?
- ☐ loo roll
- ☐ big spider
- ☐ small spider

Answers: 1. U-bend; 2. porcelain 3. big spider (well, you do in my house!)

FURZE

AAAARGH

5th WORLD RECORD

pants!

MY LOO-DICROUSLY FAST 50-MPH TOILET!

This wasn't just any 'bog standard' invention. Here I am reaching 53.25mph to set a Guinness World Record for the fastest toilet! Get in!

Push this red button and water flushes out of the back of the toilet. Awesome!

A 140cc engine with sixteen-brake horsepower to boost it along!

The electronic gear changes work perfectly – that's supercar-style toilet tech!

VROOM VROOM!

Don't use this brush for cleaning – it's in disguise as a manual gear lever!

The modified exhaust points upwards and the gases blast the loo roll round like a crazy Catherine wheel!

The toilet cost £119.90, which is about £18,000 cheaper than a Ford Focus car. Proper bargain, that!

It's not road legal, so pleeeease don't call the cops if you see me driving down your street.

FURZE

FURZE

FURZE

AKESPEARE
NTY RACEWAY

OPIE

On a drag-strip speed test I rocketed to 53.25mph. That's 11mph faster than the previous world record and Guinness World Record number five, thanks very much!

5

53·25

POSSIBLE FUTURE TOILET INVENTIONS...?

1. Toilet rollercoaster ride

2. Remote-controlled talking Portaloo

POO?

3. Lightweight toilet rucksack

Why was the detective on the toilet? Cos he wanted to get to the **bottom** of things!

125

WORLD'S FASTEST DODGEM!

In 2017, I set my sixth world record
... with a little help from a thing
called The Stig.

I say 'thing' cos no one knows exactly
what or who The Stig is, or where he
comes from. Not that it really matters –
all that does matter is that the *Top Gear*
driver blasted my special dodgem car to
100mph! That meant I got another framed
piece of paper from the Guinness World
Record bods to stick with my other five!

Why create a dodgem that moves at 100mph?

Why not?! Actually, the people at BBC
who make *Top Gear* challenged me to
convert an old fairground dodgem car into
a machine that could top 100mph.
'No problem!' I shouted back at them.

My 30-second guide to building a
100-mph dodgem car:

- *Take a battered old dodgem car
  (which you may know as a bumper
  car) from the 1960s.*

- *Remove the old chassis and base,
  and replace with a lighter chassis
  and some chunky go-kart wheels.*

- *Bung in a 600-cc engine from a
  sporty motorbike.*

- *Put the body and seat in – plus a
  shiny new exhaust pipe!*

6th WORLD RECORD

FURZE'S FAST FACT!
The original speed of the dilapidated dodgem was about 5mph, so I made it go 20 times faster than when it was ridden around at fairgrounds all those years ago!

Once I'd done all of the above, the final thing left for me to do was to take my dodgem to a top-secret, classified, mystery airfield* and let The Stig race it. I'm glad to say he recorded a speed of **100.336mph**, which left me speechless and amazed and with my sixth world record!

* It was actually at Bentwaters airfield in Suffolk, near Ipswich, off the B1069 between Rendlesham and Tunstall.

MORE WORLD RECORDS?!?

Setting world records is addictive and I'd definitely like to do more of it in the future. It's one of the things that I'm most well known for. But, any world records I attempt have to be just right for me - I'm hardly going to stand with a snooker cue on my head for two days, am I?

A few years ago, I took my Pulse-jet Kart, which is the noisiest thing I've ever created, and stuck it on the cliffs at Dover, on the south coast of England. Since the pulse-jet sounds a bit like a massive, continuous fart, the idea was that the 'fart' could be heard across the Channel in France. I should also mention that I made a big bum shape to go round the end of the jet! We think the noise was heard in France, but it was never certain, so it wasn't an official record. But maybe making something noisy that can be heard about 21 miles away is something I could do. I like a bit of noise, as you know.

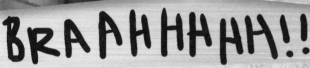

BRAAHHHHH!!

One thing I won't be doing is setting a world record for having the most world records! Some American dude called Ashrita Furman has set over 500 ridiculous records, including:

- **Most eggs crushed with toes in 30 seconds (42 eggs)**

- **Most forward rolls in one hour (1,330 rolls)**

- **Balancing a bicycle on your chin (2 minutes 1.45 seconds)**

- **Most baked beans eaten with a cocktail stick in five minutes (271 beans)**

How nuts is that? Actually, if I combined the baked beans and the farting pulse-jet noise idea, I could be on to something!!!

Fastest mile – while balancing a baseball bat on one finger!

129

SELF-WEDGIE SYSTEM

For those of you who don't know what a 'wedgie' is, I've looked in my dictionary (again!) to find this helpful definition for you:

wedgie (*noun*): the act of pulling up the material of someone's underwear, or the top of their trousers, as a joke.

You got that now? Giving someone a wedgie was a light-hearted joke when I was at school, so I've come up with the super Self-wedgie System so you can now give yourself one. All you need to do is attach the hook to the belt loop on your jeans and pull the rope. Not that you'd probably ever want to wedgie yourself, but just in case.

WHAT'S IT FOR?

Are you not paying attention?! This invention lets you give yourself a wedgie!

COME ON - IT MUST DO SOMETHING ELSE?

Ah, OK . . . it's a clever pulley-lifting device, meaning you can lift a really heavy thing just by attaching the hook to it and pulling on the cord or rope. The pulleys take the weight. I'll even reveal how you could pull yourself up.

WHAT WILL YOU NEED?

⚙ Five or six washing-line pulleys. You should be able to get them from a DIY shop. If you can't, they can be bought online.

⚙ About 10 metres of strong nylon cord or thin rope.

⚙ Twelve straight metal brackets, with three or four holes in them.

⚙ Twelve M6 bolts and nuts.

⚙ Twelve washers.

TOP TIP!

Although the pulleys are strong and robust, the cord that you use also needs to be strong enough to support the weight of whatever you lift. String and cotton are no use here, ladies and gentlemen!

ADULT SUPER VISION NEEDED

STEP 1

I'm assuming you're using five pulleys, like I did. (You can use two, but your pulling power won't be as great.) Your washing-line pulleys will probably come with a large hook attached. You can take this out, but there's a good chance you'll need an adult's help to remove it. Set the removed hooks aside.

STEP 2

Take two of the metal brackets and place them across the top and bottom of two of the pulleys, lining the holes up with the holes on the pulleys.

STEP 3

Place the bolts through the top and bottom of the brackets. Before you place nuts on the four bolts used, place two more brackets over the bolts so the pulleys get sandwiched between the brackets, then add nuts and washers. The hole on the pulley that the bolt is through might be wide, in which case a washer will help stop the bolt from moving.

STEP 4

Add two more brackets creating a V shape that will form the point where the hook will be attached. Thread two bolts through and add nuts and washers.

STEP 5

Tighten the nuts with two 10-mm spanners as shown.

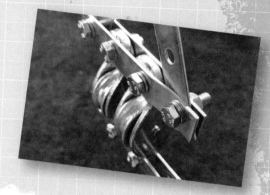

STEP 6

Maybe have a biscuit now? I'm quite keen on Bourbons!

Yum!

STEP 7

Using three more pulleys and six brackets, make the top part of the invention in the same way using bolts, nuts and washers. This time the two brackets that make a triangle shape for the hook will point upwards and will need to be fixed into the point where the pulleys are.

STEP 8

Using the hooks that you removed from the pulleys in Step 1, attach them to the top bracket and bottom bracket, like this.

STEP 9

Now it's time to thread the cord, which is dead easy. Keep one end of the cord on the floor. Take the other end and thread it through the top of the pulley, on the curved metal bit. Pull it down through the pulley, as shown. Take the end back to the top pulley and thread it through the middle pulley.

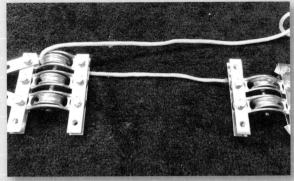

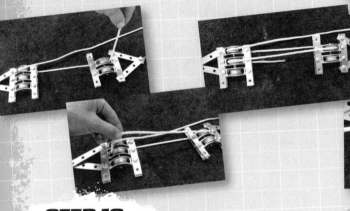

STEP 10

Repeat this until you've threaded the cord through all five pulleys. Finish by tying the cord strongly around one of the brackets at the bottom.

STEP 11

Now you need to attach the top hook safely to something, so that the whole device hangs up. Attach a heavy object to the bottom hook and pull the free end of the cord – the object should lift up! Make sure whatever you attach the top hook to can take the weight.

INVENTION 6 INVENTION

EXPERIMENT WITH IT

Before you rig up all five pulleys, try it with just two - one at the top and one at the bottom, obviously! This way you'll understand how it goes together, how the cord runs through and what weights it can pick up. You can put the pulleys, brackets and hooks in place, bolt them together and muck about with it, then undo the bolts and add more pulleys if you want to.

PULLING POWER!!!

The best thing I've done with the Self-wedgie System is pull myself up (not by my pants!) I had a big builder bag, the sort that a crane drops off with sand or soil in it. These bags hold a lot of weight! I gathered the handles together, hooked them over the hook on my pulley system, attached it to the top of the swing in my garden and pulled the cord... Amazingly, it pulled me up!

TOP TIP!
Pull the cord in a downward direction. If you pull it out to the side, the Self-wedgie System won't work so well.

••RATING••

STRENGTH: ⚙⚙⚙⚙⚙⚙⚙⚙⚙⚙

DETAIL: ⚙⚙⚙⚙⚙⚙⚙⚙⚙⚙

DIFFICULTY: ⚙⚙⚙⚙⚙⚙⚙⚙⚙⚙⚙

NOISE

This one's obvious, isn't it? Jet engines, fireworks, drums, loud speakers, rock music – I like ear-bashing stuff!

FIRE

Fire is a 'hot' favourite for me. Flames, sparks, flares, blazes and infernos are all really rather splendid.

VIEWS

As in YouTube views (the number of times people watch my videos), NOT as in views across a spring meadow with daffodils . . .

SMELL OF AN OPEN FIRE

See the 'fire' bit on this page!

SAUSAGE AND MASH

A cracking, traditional British meal. My neighbours know I love it and sometimes even bring round a plate of sausage and mash for me! Woohoo!

MOTORBIKES

I've made and modified a few of these, from flame-throwing mopeds to motorbike-powered, four-wheeled toilets!

BMX

Riding BMX bikes was the best thing in my teenage years. BMX means 'bicycle motorcross', not 'Buy More Xmas presents' as you might try to tell your parents.

ONLINE SHOPPING

I hate spending ages in shops choosing things like clothes. Internet shopping is amazing - except for when you order stuff in the wrong size and have to faff around sending it back.

DISHWASHERS

I used to think I preferred washing up, but then we got a dishwasher and it makes life so much easier. Dishwashers still don't clean things very well, though!

AND DISLIKES!

CROWDS

I try to avoid busy, crowded places. I'd much rather be in my shed or the middle of a field riding something at 60mph . . . as long as the wind isn't blowing.

WORM MUD

Hear me out on this. I get worm mud all over my garden and then it ends up inside on the floors in my house. Pesky worms.

WIND

It's just a pain. I don't mind the cold, but when I'm outside trying to do something in the wind it really riles me. It's only good for flying a kite!

RUST

It annoys me how rain and water team up as bad guys to rust metal. Using stainless steel is the answer!

TRAFFIC JAMS

They're just such a waste of time. I'm not very patient, and I hate sitting still.

CLOTHES SHOPPING

See 'Online Shopping' on the other page!

MIXING FOODS

I'm quite a neat and tidy person. I don't like it if, for example, the peas on my plate get mixed up with the mash, or if the chicken gets squashed with the carrots. Grrrr!

TOMATOES

Can't stand them. When I have pizza it just has cheese on it. My pizzas are basically cheese on toast!

DISHWASHERS

If you've paid attention, you'll have noticed dishwashers are also one of my 'likes'. But I'm not sure if I like or dislike them - perhaps they should go in the middle?!

How to:
REMOVE WIRE CASING

This may sound complicated, but it isn't; it's simply removing a little of the coloured plastic casing that goes around the outside of wire. This leaves the wire inside exposed and means it can be connected to other wire or a battery, for example. For the Remote-control Hosepipe Pranker and Auto Dart-blaster Firing System, you'll have to do a little bit of wire stripping.

1 Chances are you won't have a pair of automatic wire strippers - a tool that cleverly clamps to wire, cuts through the casing and neatly strips the casing away. Not a problem - just grab your trusty pliers!

2 Hold the wire and, at the point you want to strip back, make a very light nip with the pliers. You need to do this delicately, so that you cut the casing but not the actual wire inside.

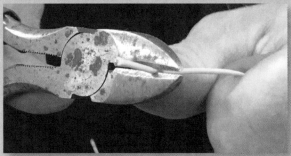

3 When you've cut through the plastic, slowly slide your pliers to the end and the plastic should come away, leaving the wire exposed. You may be able to pull the plastic away with your hand.

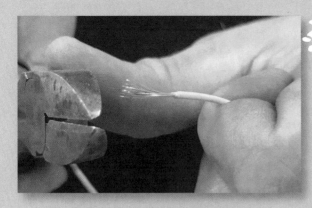

4 Sometimes, it's easier to make two or three small cuts along the plastic and then pull the casing away. This may depend on the length of wire you're trying to expose.

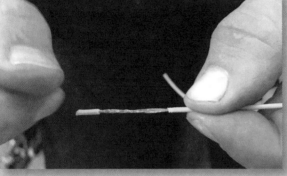

TOP TIP!

Before you slide the cut casing off completely, leave it on the end of the wire and twist it round a few times. This twists the wire neatly.

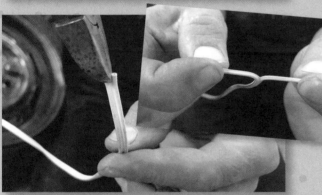

5 With twin core cable, you'll need to separate the two cores before stripping the casing. Use the end of your pliers to make a small cut between the two cores. Then, gently peel the two apart to the length you need.

Think of cutting into the wire casing as being a bit like biting a sausage roll. The casing is the light pastry bit that's easy to chomp, but the sausage inside (like the wire) is a little tougher. When you're stripping wire, the trick is not to damage the sausage!

This is making me hungry again!

REMOTE-CONTROL HOSEPIPE PRANKER

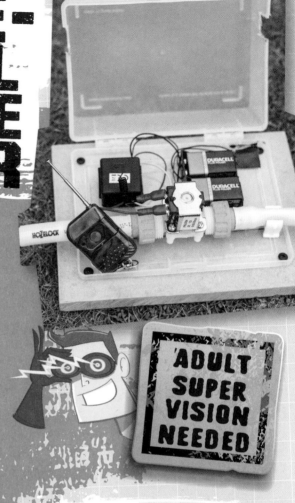

Now, I love ALL ten inventions in my book. Of course I do. They are ALL brilliantly, fabulously, spectacularly amazing in their own way. But I must say I have a soft spot for my Remote-control Hosepipe Pranker Controller Doo-daah Thingy (Remote-control Hosepipe Pranker for short!). It has basic wiring, batteries and valves inside, and you may need to buy these on the internet. But don't be scared – it's as easy to make as a cup of tea! Speaking of cups of tea, I'm off for a brew . . .

ADULT SUPER VISION NEEDED

Mmmm, that was a lovely cuppa! Right, where was I? Oh yes, my cool Hosepipe Pranker. I guarantee you'll love this as much as I do. Now read this bit, please!

WHAT'S IT FOR?

Unless you want to be able to water your mum and dad's roses and daffodils automatically, at just the push of a button, then this device is the ultimate way to prank an unsuspecting neighbour, friend, visitor . . . or postman or woman! Just get the Remote-control Hosepipe Pranker in place in your garden or outside your house, hide somewhere, press the button and your target will be squirted with water!

H_2Ohhhhh, that's funny!

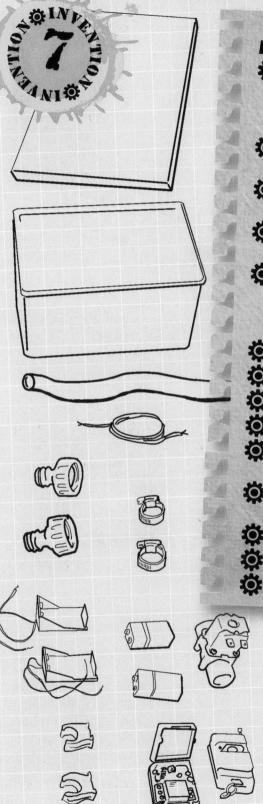

WHAT WILL YOU NEED?

⚙ A 12-volt ¾-inch BSP solenoid valve. You can buy these online, usually for four or five quid. In the item description, make sure it says the valve is 'normally closed' or 'NC'.

⚙ Two 9-volt batteries. These are the common rectangular batteries that loads of shops sell.

⚙ Two 9-volt battery holders, with wiring attached.

⚙ About 50cm of low-voltage wiring. Speaker wire (which is twin core) is best.

⚙ A 12-volt remote-control transmitter and receiver. (See photo opposite.) Again, you can get one of these online for about a fiver from a DIY store.

⚙ Two 15-mm plumbing pipe clips.

⚙ Several small screws.

⚙ Two ¾-inch hosepipe connectors.

⚙ Standard hosepipe. You'll need two pieces.

⚙ A block of wood about 20–30cm long and 20cm wide.

⚙ A plastic lunchbox or tub with a lid. See page 142. (This is not so you can have a sandwich!)

⚙ Black tape or insulation tape.

⚙ Junior hacksaw.

⚙ Two Jubilee Clips.

VIDEO ALERT!
There's a video of me making the Remote-control Hosepipe Pranker. Go to: **www.puffin.co.uk/colin-furze** and you'll see me putting this beauty together, step by step.

STEP 1

Start with the plastic lunchbox or tub. This is going to have everything inside it: the solenoid valve, batteries, clips and whatnot. Place the lid upside down in the centre of the block of wood and drill a pilot hole in each corner. Now screw the lid to the wood.

TOP TIP!

When the lid is closed, you need to be able to open the lunchbox again easily. Some lunchboxes are tricky to open when they're closed and upside down, so choose your lunchbox carefully.

TOP TIP!

On the bottom of the solenoid valve is an arrow. This shows you which way the water will flow through it and out of your bits of hosepipe.

STEP 2

Screw your hosepipe connectors on to each end of the solenoid valve. Line the valve and connectors up near the long edge of the lunchbox lid (the edge furthest away from the box) but in a position where the box will still close. Make a mark with a pen in line with the pointy bit of one of the connectors.

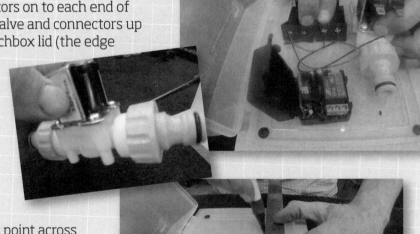

STEP 3

Draw a straight line from this point across the lid.

INVENTION 7

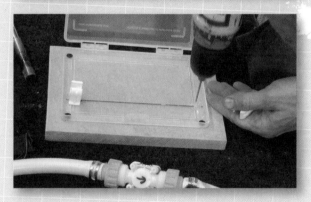

STEP 4

Attach one piece of hosepipe to each of the connectors. Firmly push the hosepipe over the connector, then slide a Jubilee Clip over each pipe and leave it at the exact spot where the pipe connects with the connector. When you tighten the screw on the Jubilee Clip, it'll clamp the pipe to the connector.

STEP 5

It's time to fix the 15-mm plumbing pipe clips at each end of the line you've drawn. Make sure they are in the right position as they need to hold the hosepipe in place. Hold one clip on the line and make a mark on the lid through the hole in the middle of the clip. This mark is where you need to drill a pilot hole. Screw the pipe clip in, then do the same with the other clip on the other end.

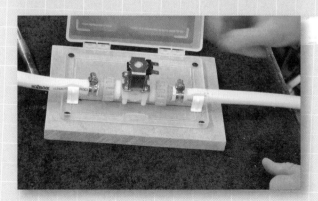

STEP 6

Push the hosepipe in to each plumbing clip, with the solenoid valve in the middle.

STEP 7

Get the box part of the remote-control switch and carefully lift out the circuit board and bits and pieces inside it – these should easily come out all together. Screw the box to the lid in this position.

STEP 8

Hold the box in place and carefully drill a pilot hole through the box and partly into the wood. Keep your fingers clear of the drill. Screw the box to the lid of the lunchbox. Take a small piece of black tape or insulation tape and stick it over the screw. This stops the metal screw from interfering with the metal bits on the circuit board. Put the circuit board back in the box.

STEP 9

You need to get the two 9-volt battery holders in place now. Look at this picture to see roughly where they should go. They need to be near enough to the remote-control switch so that the wires will connect.

Counter-sink the holes in the battery holders so the screw heads won't get in the way of the batteries.

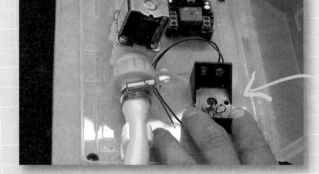

STEP 10

Each battery holder has a red cable and a black cable. The red is known as the 'positive' cable and the black is the 'negative' cable. Take the red from one of the holders and the black from the other. Strip about 2cm of wire casing from each of these and twist the exposed metal together. Wrap a small piece of black tape around the end.

In the YouTube video I show you how to do this easily, so check it out!

STEP 11

Now look closely at the circuit board. There's a small hole with a '+' (positive) sign and another with a '-' (negative) sign. Thread the end of the other red wire into the positive hole, then tighten the small screw above it with a screwdriver. Do the same with the other black wire into the negative hole.

STEP 12

You'll see there are also small holes on the circuit board marked 'NC' (normally closed) and 'NO' (normally open). Take a separate small length of wire and put it in the NC hole and tighten the screw.

TOP TIP!

Some boards require an extra live wire to be connected to the COM port, which usually sits between NC and NO.

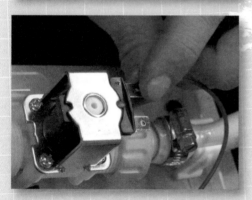

STEP 13

Connect the other end of this wire to either of the terminals on the solenoid valve. You'll need to strip a little of the wire casing off, thread the wire through the little metal hole and wrap it around.

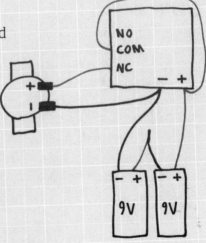

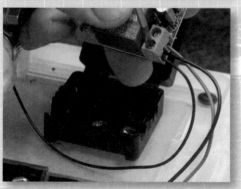

STEP 14

Take another piece of wire and connect it to the other terminal on the valve. This needs to go to the negative hole (that's the one with the '-' sign) on the board. Unscrew the screw above the negative hole and put this wire in the hole, as well as the wire that originally went into the same hole from the battery holder. You'll now have two wires going into the same negative hole. Tighten the screw.

STEP 15

Put the 9-volt batteries in each of the holders, then put the circuit board back in its little box and close the lid on the remote-control switch.

STEP 16

As you now have wires coming from the remote-control switch, its lid might not close and you may need to carefully snip off the plastic lugs on the lid with pliers so that it shuts.

STEP 17

Nearly done! When you try to close the lunchbox lid, the hosepipe on either side will stop it from closing. Close the lid as far as you can. Then, mark the box where you need to cut a hole in each side to allow the pipe to come out and the lid to close. Cut the holes.

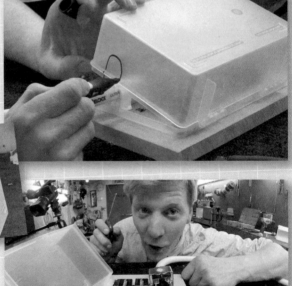

Use a junior hacksaw to carefully cut through the plastic. Using pliers may split the plastic.

STEP 18

Before connecting it up to the tap, test that everything is working. You should hear a click from the solenoid valve when you press the remote-control button.

STEP 19

Connect one end of the Remote-control Hosepipe Pranker to your outside tap, position the other end somewhere in your garden. Making sure the tap is turned on, push the button on the remote control and watch the water burst out!

-CLICK-

FSSHHH!!!

SSSHHHH!!

••RATING••

STRENGTH:
DETAIL:
DIFFICULTY:

What if I Made a JOKE-O-MATIC Machine?!

Speaking of pranks, I've already invented the Cake-O-Matic, which blasts out chocolate sponge faster than Usain Bolt with jet-powered shoes! But what if I could create a Joke-O-Matic and have amazing gags and laughs churned out at super speed?! I'm not sure how that would actually work (and it'll never happen, of course), so I guess you'll just have to make do with these slightly cheesy jokes and laughs instead . . .

What do you call a vicar on a motorbike?
Rev!

What do you call a fly without wings?
'A walk!

Why do bees have sticky hair?
Because they use honeycombs!

Which animal needs to wear a wig?
'A bald eagle!

When do you know a scarecrow is doing a good job?
When he's been outstanding in his field!

What did the Spanish firefighter name his twin sons?
José and Hose B!

Knock, knock
Who's there?
Figs.
Figs who?
Figs the doorbell, it's broken!

My friend asked me to do odd jobs for him around his house. He gave me a list of ten jobs . . .
I did 1, 3, 5, 7, and 9.

How do inventors freshen their breath?
With experi-mints!

What do you call a laughing motorbike?
A Yamaha-ha-ha-ha-ha-ha!

How do you cut the sea in two?
With a 'sea' saw!

How do you get straight As?
Use a ruler!

Knock, knock
Who's there?
Europe.
Europe who?
No, YOU'RE a poo!

What happened after the wheel was invented?
A revolution!

149

AUTO DART-BLASTER FIRING SYSTEM

Chances are you already have a dart-blaster toy a bit like this knocking around. They're great fun, and even though I'm about three times older than most people who have them, I think they're awesome! And I'm about to show you how you can make a toy like this even more awesome!

POW! POW!

ADULT SUPER VISION NEEDED

INVENTION 8

WHAT'S IT FOR?

The Auto Dart-blaster Firing System is a clever device that shoots foam darts from your toy while you hide and press the button! How cooooool is that?!*

*Answer: Mega cooooool!

VIDEO ALERT!

There's a video of me making the Auto Dart-blaster Firing System. Go to: www.puffin.co.uk/colin-furze to view it.

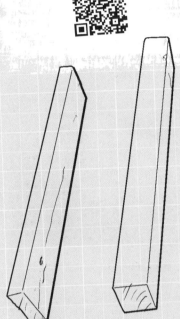

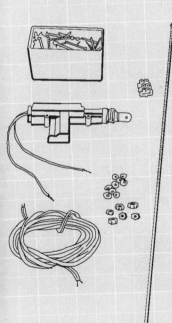

WHAT WILL YOU NEED?

- ⚙ A dart-blaster toy. It doesn't have to be exactly like the one I've used but, if you can, get one that's fairly big and shoots lots of foam darts.

- ⚙ Some wood. Try to use decent-quality, fairly thick, soft pine wood—this can be bought quite easily and cheaply from DIY shops. You'll probably want around two metres.

- ⚙ A thinner piece of wood, ideally around 2cm wide and 2cm high. The length of this piece will depend on how long your dart-blaster toy is, and I'll talk about that in a bit.

- ⚙ Some normal wood screws, nuts and washers.

- ⚙ A 12-volt central locking actuator. See Steps 6–8 to see what this looks like. You'll need to buy this online. It should be around £5.

- ⚙ Two 9-volt batteries and two 9-volt battery-holder clips.

- ⚙ About one metre of speaker cable. Most DIY shops sell this. If you know someone who has had a surround sound TV system installed, they might have some spare speaker cable you could use.

- ⚙ A long M4 threaded bar.

- ⚙ A 12-volt push-button momentary switch. When you buy this in an electrical shop or online, check that the two little metal spades that stick out from the opposite end to the button have holes in them.

- ⚙ Cable-connector block.

- ⚙ Jubilee Clips or zip/cable ties.

- ⚙ Tape, string and a pen or pencil.

- ⚙ Cardboard tube.

- ⚙ Drill and drill bit.

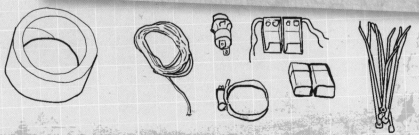

STEP 1

First, make the base to support your dart-blaster. You need two lengths of wood about 30cm long and three lengths 20cm long. Lay the 30-cm pieces 20cm apart and lay the 20-cm pieces across them – one at each end, and the third exactly in the middle.

STEP 2

Drill pilot holes, countersink and screw these five pieces together.

STEP 3

Your 20- by 20-mm wood needs to be as long as the length of your dart-blaster, plus around another 20cm, so that the 12-volt actuator can attach to the end of it. Measure your wood, and cut to size if necessary.

STEP 4

Attach the 20- by 20-mm wood to the side of your blaster, using zip/cable ties or Jubilee Clips.

TOP TIP!

You may need to screw a small screw to the side of the wood that's in contact with the toy, leaving the tip of the screw sticking out. This can help to balance the wood and keep it straight – look at the YouTube video of me building this invention to see what I mean.

STEP 5

The holes on either side of your 12-volt actuator need to be slightly bigger. Using a 4-mm drill bit, carefully drill through them. Your M4 threaded bar will now fit through the holes.

STEP 6

The actuator must be fixed to the end of your wood and held in a position roughly in line with the trigger of your blaster (and pointing the same way). With the threaded bar in one of the holes, hold the actuator where you want to fix it, then mark this point on the bar. (Flick to page 158 to see how to saw metal with a hacksaw.) Saw another length of the bar for the other hole in the actuator.

STEP 7

Mark the position on the wood where each bar will line up, then drill holes for the bar to go through with a 4-mm drill bit.

STEP 8

Push the bars into the holes in the actuator. Put a nut and washer on each end of the bars, sandwiching the actuator in place on the bars.

STEP 9

Place two nuts and two washers further down the two bars, hold the actuator in a position that's in line with the toy's trigger. Push the bars through the holes in the wood and put a nut and washer on the very top of each bar.

STEP 10

Hold the dart-blaster up with two fingers to find its balancing point. This is where you'll attach a thick piece of wood to the long, thin piece. The wood going to the base must be around 10cm longer than the depth of the blaster. Screw this to the long, thin piece.

STEP 11

Screw the thick piece you've just attached to the centre of your wooden base.

INVENTION INVENTION
INVENTION INVENTION

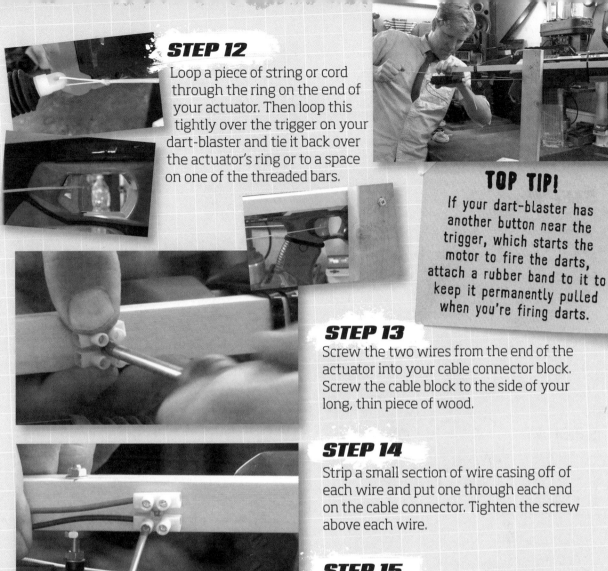

STEP 12

Loop a piece of string or cord through the ring on the end of your actuator. Then loop this tightly over the trigger on your dart-blaster and tie it back over the actuator's ring or to a space on one of the threaded bars.

TOP TIP!

If your dart-blaster has another button near the trigger, which starts the motor to fire the darts, attach a rubber band to it to keep it permanently pulled when you're firing darts.

STEP 13

Screw the two wires from the end of the actuator into your cable connector block. Screw the cable block to the side of your long, thin piece of wood.

STEP 14

Strip a small section of wire casing off of each wire and put one through each end on the cable connector. Tighten the screw above each wire.

STEP 15

Screw the battery-holders to the middle of the arm of your wooden base. Take a red wire from one and connect that to the black wire of the other one. Twist the exposed wires of each together so that they are joined, then tape this connection to the wooden arm.

STEP 16

The speaker wire has two cables joined together. One end of each wire needs to go in the connector screwed to the wood. Carefully pull the wire apart, strip the casing off and screw into the holes.

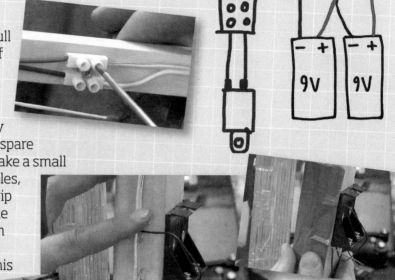

STEP 17

Hold this cable next to the battery holders, giving yourself plenty of spare length in the cable. With pliers, make a small cut in the casing of one of the cables, split the cable back about 5cm, strip the end of each wire and twist one of the ends to the black cable from the battery-holder, and the other to the end of the red wire. Tape this connection to the wooden arm.

STEP 18

With the other end of the speaker wire, strip a little of each plastic casing and thread one bit of wire through each hole in the push button, then twist the wire round.

TOP TIP!

If the invention doesn't work when it's connected up, you may need to switch the cable wires that go into the connector. Undo the screws, put each wire into the other end and tighten again.

STEP 19

Cut a cardboard tube down the long side, place your switch tightly inside it and wrap some tape around the tube. Put the batteries in the holders, load up your dart-blaster with foam darts, press the button ... and your Auto Dart-blaster Firing System is ready to rock!

Oooohhh, you're gonna love this! Now that you've constructed your Auto-dart Blaster Firing System (ADBFS for short, if you (ike) you can carefully position this page somewhere and use it for target practice! What will you score?

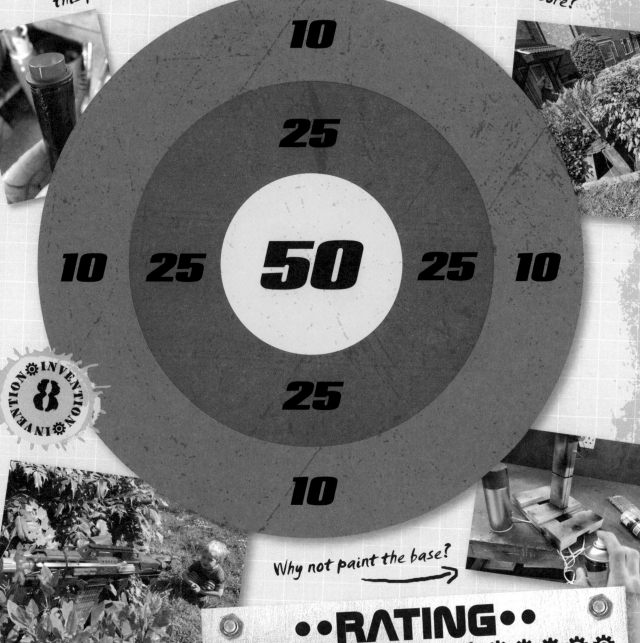

INVENTION 8

10

25

10   25   **50**   25   10

25

10

Why not paint the base? →

••RATING••

STRENGTH: ⚙⚙⚙⚙⚙⚙⚙⚙⚙⚙

DETAIL: ⚙⚙⚙⚙⚙⚙⚙⚙⚙⚙

DIFFICULTY: ⚙⚙⚙⚙⚙⚙⚙⚙⚙⚙

How to:
SAW METAL

The method for sawing metal is similar to sawing wood, but you use a different saw and need to be aware of a few things. You'll be cutting metal for your Bike-wheel Fire Vortex (that's on page 160 - how exciting!) and invention number ten - the Downhill Racer.

ADULT SUPER VISION NEEDED

1 When you're cutting the metal brackets for your Downhill Racer, you'll need to clamp them in a vice. Metal is usually thinner and smaller than wood, and is tricky to hold in place with one hand while you saw with the other. Plus, it's much harder work and you may need two hands on your saw!

TOP TIP!
If you don't have a vice to hold the metal, you could fix it to a raised wooden surface using bolts, nuts and washers like this.

2 You'll need to use a bigger saw, like this, which is different from the saw you've used to cut wood. It has a thin blade with lots of small, sharp teeth. Use a pencil to mark a line on the metal where you need to saw.

3 Slowly move the saw backwards and forward along the pencil line, using the whole length of the blade.

4 The angle you saw the metal at can be lower than the position you use to saw wood. This is because the metal saw's blade is a lot finer and can work at a lower angle.

for wood

for metal

*I know tennis rackets have lots of little holes, but I mean one HUGE hole!

BIKE-WHEEL FIRE VORTEX

Now things are really going to heat up! I'm well known for using fire, flames and burny things in my creations. I also want to show you how you can incorporate flames into one of the inventions in this book - but in a safe and sensible way, of course.

Here are some ESSENTIAL things for you to know and do before you begin this exciting build.

1 An adult must **always** be with you to supervise when you're making and operating the Bike-wheel Fire Vortex.

2 Only an adult can light whatever you burn on the wheel.

3 Always stay away from the fire.

4 Have a fire extinguisher nearby at all times.

I know it's not usually like me to be so serious, but fire is serious!

WHAT WILL IT DO?

It's a simple invention, but very cool. When something is lit and placed on the tray on the wheel, you turn the pedal to spin the wheel and create a twisty fire vortex. This invention serves no other purpose than to create a mini fire vortex. Excellent!

FIRE FOR MY FOUR MILLIONTH SUBSCRIBER!

In early 2017, when I hit four million subscribers on my YouTube channel, I celebrated by making a giant fire vortex. The flame was as big as a house and I stuck firework rockets on the top! But please do not try this at home!

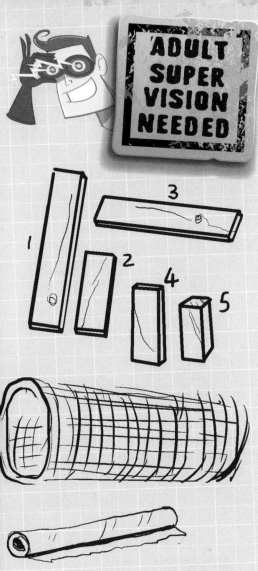

WHAT WILL YOU NEED?

⚙ An old bike. Well, the back part of an old bike! You'll need the wheels to be fairly big and it's easier if it doesn't have gears. Save the front for Invention 10.

⚙ Five thick pieces of wood at different lengths (more details to follow).

⚙ A Jubilee Clip.

⚙ Chicken wire with small holes (this is wire mesh with squares in it that's used to make little wire fences and stuff like that). You should be able to buy this at a DIY or hardware shop. I'll tell you how much you'll need in the steps.

⚙ Turkey foil tray or enough thick tinfoil to cover a whole wheel and a small, foil tray about 1/3 of the size of the wheel.

⚙ Large hacksaw.

⚙ A few screws.

⚙ Optional – plastic tyre lever (if you have one).

⚙ Cable ties and gloves for handling wire and foil.

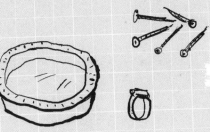

handlebars

top tube

seat tube

seat-stay

down tube

chain-ring

gears

axle

chain-stay

crank

pedal

STEP 1

Start with the bike. Take your large hacksaw and begin carefully sawing through the top tube and the down tube, close to the seat tube. You only need the rear part of the bike for this invention – save the front for Invention Ten!

If the bike isn't yours, make sure you have permission to saw it in half!

STEP 2

Remove the back brake. Use the hacksaw to saw through the chain-stay and seat-stay bits of metal (see diagram on page 161) on the side of the bike that doesn't have the crank and chain. This is to create the space to attach your chicken wire. Remove the nut and bolt from the side of the wheel that the chain-stay and seat-stay are attached to, and the stays should come away.

TOP TIP!

Cut the chain-stay and seat-stay on the side opposite the chain – look at this picture:

STEP 3

Take the tyre off of the wheel. You can use a flathead screwdriver to get into the wheel rim and prise the tyre off, but it's much better to use a plastic tyre lever. These clever tools come with all standard puncture-repair kits, and usually have instructions on how to remove a tyre properly.

STEP 4

You need to raise the bike up on wooden supports, so that when the pedals turn, they don't touch the ground. Lay out the wood like the picture on the right. Measure between the centre of the wheel and the centre of the seat tube (the red line in the picture on the left). This needs to be the width across one of your bits of wood as shown.

STEP 5

Lay your bike over this funny 'h-shaped' wood layout, using something like two paint cans to prop the bike up. Measure from the bike frame vertically to the wooden base and cut a piece of wood this length.

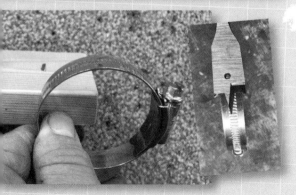

STEP 6

Drill a wide hole through the top of the support piece you've just cut, big enough to fit the Jubilee Clip through. You may need to drill a few holes together to make one big, wide hole.

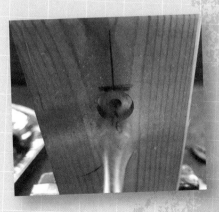

STEP 7

Line up the upright piece of wood under your seat-stay and frame, in a position that won't interfere with the pedal when it's turned. Ensure that the axle for the wheel of the bike will be above the position indicated here. Screw the upright piece of wood to the base. Then, rest the frame on top and loop the Jubilee Clip through the wide hole in the wood to secure the frame to the upright piece.

STEP 8

Now measure the distance under the wheel to the wooden base on the ground and cut a piece of wood this length. This will be used to raise the wheel up. Drill a hole in the top of this piece slightly bigger than the axle sticking out from the wheel. The wheel's axle is the bit poking out furthest from the chain area, and it will rest in this hole and stop the wheel moving about. Balance the bike in the hole to check the positioning of the second upright piece, mark with a pencil on the base, and screw this to the base.

STEP 9

Your bike will now be raised on wooden supports over the base, letting you turn the pedal. Tighten the Jubilee Clip and secure it in place.

STEP 10

Put on your gloves and take the turkey tray or thick foil and cover the wheel, poking the bolt sticking up through the centre of the wheel through. Trim off any overhanging bits. Use tape to secure it to the spokes underneath.

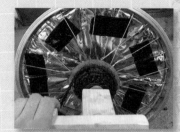

STEP 11

Add the small foil tray as shown, pushing the bolt through the centre. This will hold the tray in place when the wheel is turning.

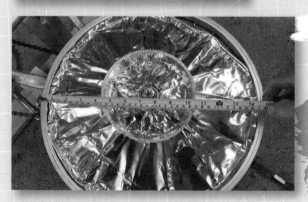

TOP TIP!

The tray needs to cover approximately one third of the wheel's area, so don't use a tray that's way too big or too tiny.

STEP 12

Now add the chicken wire. Here's a maths bit to show you how much you'll need …

MATHS BIT

Measure the diameter of the wheel, then multiply it by Pi. No, not 'pie' as in steak and kidney, but 'Pi' as in the ancient formula discovered by some clever Greek bloke. Pi is 3.14159 (roughly), so if the wheel diameter is 20cm, you'll need about 62.831cm of chicken wire (20 x 3.14159). Maths bit over, folks!

STEP 13

Still wearing gloves, cut your chicken wire to the desired length to go around the circumference of the wheel, adding about 20mm that you can use to overlap. Use a strong pair of pliers and be **very careful** of any sharp pieces of metal sticking out.

TOP TIP!

The chicken wire should be about twice the height of the wheel's diameter.

STEP 14

You can attach the wire to the edge of the wheel using cable ties. Attach a cable tie to the top at the point where your chicken wire overlaps. Keep your gloves on to handle the chicken wire.

Keep those gloves on!

STEP 15

Test to see if the wheel spins freely. If the pedal underneath gets caught, then you can remove it. If it's still getting in the way you can cut off the crank. The crank is very tough to saw, so only do this if absolutely needed!

STEP 16

Ask an adult to find a safe place outside for the vortex and then they can carefully light a small piece of unwanted material and drop it on to the tray. Start turning the pedal and you'll begin to create your Bike-wheel Fire Vortex. Congrats!

LIGHT FIRE OUTSIDE ONLY!
Fires inside can cause deadly carbon monoxide poisoning.

whooff!

COLIN'S CHALLENGE
Now that you've made it, you'll need to experiment in the best way to 'whip up' the fire vortex. There are lots of things that can affect the flame, such as wind speed, the size of the holes in the chicken wire (smaller holes are better) and the speed you turn the pedal.

••RATING••
STRENGTH: ⚙⚙⚙⚙⚙⚙⚙⚙⚙⚙
DETAIL: ⚙⚙⚙⚙⚙⚙⚙⚙⚙⚙
DIFFICULTY: ⚙⚙⚙⚙⚙⚙⚙⚙⚙⚙

How to:
DRILL METAL

Hopefully you're comfortable drilling holes into wood now. To create the next invention - your Downhill Racer, you'll need to know how to drill holes into metal. Look over these tips to master the technique.

1 First thing's first, folks: a drill bit that's meant for drilling wood won't drill into metal. No way. You need an HSS drill bit, (that stands for 'high-speed steel'). These are usually black or silver with gold tips.

2 Mark the spot you want to drill with a permanent marker pen and put on some safety goggles.

TOP TIP!

If you have a metal punch, gently tap this with a hammer on your marked spot. (You could also use a screw.) This will make a small indent on the metal and gives the drill bit something to sit in as you start drilling.

3 If you're drilling an 8-mm hole into metal (and you will be for the Downhill Racer), drill a smaller pilot hole first with a smaller metal drill bit. Drilling an 8-mm hole – or one even bigger – without a pilot hole will be hard work!

4 Hold the drill directly in line with the point you need to drill and slowly push the drill down, just like you're drilling wood. Make sure you don't wriggle the drill around.

As a general rule, the harder the metal is, the slower your drill should spin. Remember that metal is much stronger than wood.

5 When you've drilled your pilot hole right through the metal, change the drill bit to the size you need, then drill the hole again in the same way.

TOP TIP!

Always keep your goggles on and use a dustpan and brush to sweep up the little metal filings because they may be sharp.

DOWNHILL RACER

I can't believe you're about to build the terrific tenth invention from This Book isn't Safe! On a scale of one to ten, my excitement level is at 23,456,772 right now! So far you've created crazy contraptions like the Remote-control Hosepipe Pranker and the Fab Frisbee Flinger, but you'll need all your skill and brainpower to put together your own Downhill Racer.
So let's get cracking . . .

INVENTION 10 INVENTION

ZOOOM!

WHAT'S IT FOR?

Your Downhill Racer will be an epic machine that you can sit on the back of and roll around your garden, along cycle paths or down little hills. It has a brake on the front wheel and it's fully steerable.

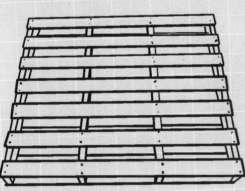

Will the postman or woman get this through your letterbox?!

WHAT WILL YOU NEED?

⚙ A small kid's bike. This could be an old bike that a three-year-old may have used. It doesn't have to be in good condition, as you only need its wheels.

⚙ A larger kid's bike. You'll be using the front end and wheel. You could use the front of the bike in Invention 9.

⚙ A wooden pallet. I recommend using a pallet that cement bags are delivered on, as these are generally good quality, but any regular-sized pallet will do. Ask a large DIY shop or building centre if they have a spare one they can lend to you.*

⚙ 1 metre of 25-mm by 3-mm angle iron. If you can't buy this locally, you can order it online and get it delivered for not too many pennies.

⚙ 1 metre of 25-mm by 3-mm flat bar iron. Again, you can buy this online and have it delivered.

⚙ Several M8-size nuts, bolts and washers.

⚙ Hammer

⚙ Sandpaper

⚙ Hacksaw

⚙ Pliers

⚙ A bit of time! This is not something you'll be able to build in a couple of hours, but that's fine. I want to show you an invention you can build that will still challenge you and make you concentrate. I guarantee you'll love it!

* I say 'lend', but the shop won't be getting it back cos you're gonna chop and bash it up!

STEP 1

Pick an end of the pallet to work from. Choose the end that is in the best condition.

STEP 2

Take the wheels off the smaller bike by undoing the nuts and carefully sliding them out.

STEP 3

Lay the wheels over the end of the pallet that you're using as the Downhill Racer's frame. From the pictures, you can see my wheels fit between planks one and four of the pallet, so I know my racer's frame can be four planks long. Saw off the other part of the pallet, but keep it for later.

STEP 4

Place your angle iron against the middle two planks of your pallet, flush against one end. Mark the other end of the iron in line with the outer edge of the second plank. Cut this section of the angle iron and repeat four times, so that you have four iron sections the same size.

STEP 5

These four bits are your wheel brackets. Mark the centre of each bracket and drill a hole in the metal so that the bolt from each wheel will go through it. Place a bracket on either side of each wheel and tighten the nuts on the outside of the bracket.

STEP 6

Carefully measure the distance from the inside edge of one bracket to the inside edge of the other for **one** of the wheels. Make a note of the measurement.

STEP 7

Pay attention now! You know the distance between the brackets when they're on the wheel you've measured, so take them off the wheel again. Place one bracket on your pallet above one of the wooden struts.

STEP 8

The other bracket must be the same distance you measured in Step 6 away from the first bracket, which means that at the moment it won't have a wooden strut running under it so there's nothing to screw it to. You need to move the end of the wood inwards, so that it is positioned under the other bracket.

STEP 9

Measure the distance from the strut under the first bracket to the second bracket (that you measured in Step 6) plus the thickness of the wood on the end that you're moving in. Mark this total distance away from the wooden strut and run a line across the four pieces of wood on both sides.

STEP 10

Now you've marked the line, you need to cut along the outer planks on both sides of pallet. The other two centre planks you can cut flush to the two struts.

STEP 11

You'll have something left over that looks like this. Don't chuck this bit away.

STEP 12

Do the same on the other side of the main pallet, but measure the distance between the angle bars on this wheel, because they may not be the same distance apart as the first wheel. You're now left with an H-shaped piece.

STEP 13

Remove the two central pieces from one side. Place one spare piece of wood between the planks, push it down and carefully ping the wood off. Remove any exposed nails with a hammer.

STEP 14

The next job is to take off the bits of wood sticking up from the ends you've just cut away. Place these over the edge of the main pallet and, using a spare piece of wood, place it at an angle on the wood and tap the wood with a hammer. The wood might split, but that's OK because you want to keep the two longer pieces.

WHACK!

STEP 15

Sand down all the wood you're using with sandpaper to tidy up any rough edges.

STEP 16

Drill and screw the long pieces of wood from Step 14 back into the main frame.

STEP 17

Take the two little bits of wood off from each end on the **top** only.

TOP TIP!

Remember that the 'top' of your Downhill Racer is where you removed the two slats from the middle so that you can kneel inside it.

STEP 18

Grab the spare piece of pallet left over from Step 3. Saw off the bigger end bit from it, and remove the top bits of wood on both sides, as in Step 17. Cut that to fit into one end of the frame at the point where you imagine its handlebars will be and slot and screw it in.

STEP 19

Remove three longer lengths on the unused pallet. Using a piece of small angle iron, place the pallet on the floor facing upwards, then put the iron over the middle. Bash it with a hammer to split the pallet. Pull the pallet in half, bash the other bits of wood away to leave three long lengths.

STEP 20

Grab four spare pieces of wood all the same width and depth and cut them to 30cm long. These need to be screwed to the front of your racer (where the bike's handlebars will be attached).

STEP 21

You need another piece of wood running across the top of these four pieces; screw it behind them, leaving a flat surface on the other side. Look at where I put the screws and put yours in the same position; when you bolt the bike to it, you don't want any screws getting in the way.

STEP 22

Stand the racer's frame up, put a long piece of wood between the planks at the back, and line it up to the top to make an angled support. Mark a line underneath this angled piece – this is where you'll saw the wood so that it sits flush at an angle. Drill and screw both ends, then do the same on the other side.

STEP 23

Cut out the centre piece out from the top so you can get in and out of the racer easily.

STEP 24

Turn the frame upside down, then get your wheels, reattach the angle irons and place them inside the gaps on each side. Draw a long line on the wood, showing where the nails are in the pallet – this shows you where to avoid drilling a hole in your angle iron as you screw the wheel brackets on. Do that on all four sides for each wheel.

STEP 25

Now that you can see where the nails are, put your wheel brackets in place and mark the point on the iron where you'll drill a hole while avoiding the nails. Drill four holes in the iron, with the iron clamped securely on a vice.

STEP 26

Using four screws, attach each wheel bracket to the racer's frame.

STEP 27

Place your larger bike on the ground. Hold the racer's frame up to the bike's top and down tube – you're working out where to cut each tube so the bike can be bolted to the wood. The racer can tilt forward a bit when it's fixed to the bike, but it can't tilt backwards. Mark the line where you'll saw through the bike's tubes. Carefully use a hacksaw to saw through the top tube and down tube along the line you marked. Using pliers, chop off the cables going to the rear brake and any gear-changing cables.

Make sure you don't chop the front brake cable, you'll need that!

STEP 28

Saw your leftover piece of angle iron into two bits that will fit the width of the wood on the front of the racer where you will fix them. Drill two holes in each angle iron like the diagram. Hold each one up to the bike's frame so they are flush with the cut on the frame, as shown. Mark where the holes touch.

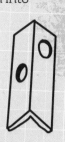

STEP 29

Drill each tube through the marks you've made. Bolt a piece of angle iron through each hole to make two brackets to attach to the wooden frame.

TOP TIP!

Try to fix two nuts on the inside of each bolt, too. When the outside nuts are tightened, the inside bolts will stop the bike tubes from moving in and crushing the metal.

STEP 30

Bolt those two brackets to the racer's frame, so the racer is in the middle of the wood.

STEP 31

Now, you need to make the angled support. With the bike bolted to the wood, measure the distance from just behind the hole you have drilled to about 40mm from the edge of the wooden frame, add 25mm to each end as these bits will become your tabs that you will drill and bend to fit up to your frame and bike.

STEP 32

Cut two flat bar iron sections to the length you've just measured. These will be attached at an angle to strengthen the racer.

STEP 33

Drill a hole in each end of the flat bar iron sections. Place one of the bars in a vice and carefully hammer, so that it bends.

TOP TIP!

If you don't have a vice, place the bar over the end of a piece of wood on the ground, hold the bar down with one hand and hit the other with a hammer so that it bends.

STEP 34

When you think you've bent each end of both bars enough, hold it up to the bike and check they'll fit and can be attached to the bike and wood with nuts and bolts easily. If you need to bend the bar more, or less, then just hit them again with the hammer until you get it right. Mark and drill holes through the down tube and the wooden frame.

STEP 35

Attach these angled supports to each side of the bike with nuts and bolts. Your amazing Downhill Racer invention is now finished – time to have some **SERIOUS** fun playing in it!

Wahey!

Kneel on a cushion!

••RATING••

STRENGTH: ⚙⚙⚙⚙⚙⚙⚙⚙⚙⚙
DETAIL: ⚙⚙⚙⚙⚙⚙⚙⚙⚙⚙
DIFFICULTY: ⚙⚙⚙⚙⚙⚙⚙⚙⚙⚙

DESIGN AND MAKE YOUR OWN INVENTIONS!

That's exactly what I want you to try now. You've built a load of inventions with my help, and I reckon you're clever and confident enough to begin thinking about your own stuff. So, what are your ideas? What tools and materials will you need? Which adult can help you? Does your invention have a whacky name? You can write down and draw some of your thoughts over the next few pages.

Some things you could build . . .

- ⚙ A cool bike stand
- ⚙ A utility belt for your TV remote, phone and games controller
- ⚙ A pulley system to open and close your curtains while you lie in bed
- ⚙ An auto-push button device for opening the drawers in your bedroom

MY INVENTION IS FOR:

....

THE THINGS I'LL NEED:

....

....

....

....

THE TOOLS I'LL NEED:

....

....

....

DIFFICULTY RATING:

....

MY INVENTION IS FOR:

....

THE THINGS I'LL NEED:

....

....

....

....

....

THE TOOLS I'LL NEED:

....

....

....

....

DIFFICULTY RATING:

....

MY INVENTION IS FOR:

....

THE THINGS I'LL NEED:

....

....

....

....

....

THE TOOLS I'LL NEED:

....

....

....

....

DIFFICULTY RATING:

....

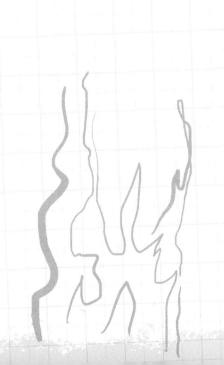

MY INVENTION IS FOR:

....

THE THINGS I'LL NEED:

....
....
....
....
....

THE TOOLS I'LL NEED:

....
....
....

DIFFICULTY RATING:

....

BYEEEEEEEE!

Good work! You've made it to the end of my book! You've screwed, drilled, bashed, measured, sawed, cut, tightened, connected and done all sorts of amazing stuff. You've used wood, metal, batteries, wire, plastic milk bottles, cement, bikes, hooks, washers, pulleys, clips and loads of other things. How amazing does that feel?!

Now that you've read every page, why not take a moment to fill in this quick questionnaire?

I think This Book Isn't Safe! is...

The best book ever to appear on Planet Earth! ☐

Full of amazing and easy-to-build inventions! ☐

Even more useful than self-cleaning underpants! ☐

Funny, like when it revealed 'Furze' means 'fart' in German! ☐

Something lots of people should read and be inspired by! ☐

Do these actually exist?! Sounds like something I should invent!

Hopefully you've ticked ALL the boxes above. As proud as I am of the fun things in my book (I'm less proud that 'Furze' means 'fart'), I really hope that it has encouraged you to get creative with tools and materials and start building and inventing things. I honestly don't do all this stuff and spend days and days in The Shed making YouTube videos for any reason other than because I absolutely enjoy it. I want to inspire people to do the same. I'm not interested in being famous – as long as people view my videos and love what I do, then I am more than happy. Whatever age you are and wherever you live, as long as you have an adult to supervise, nothing should stop you from picking up a screwdriver, a saw, a bit of wood, some metal and any other bits and bobs and dreaming up a fun creation.

I'll leave you with this simple message: Keep **thinking**, keep **inventing** and keep **challenging yourself**. *See ya!*

TICK WHAT YOU HAVE LEARNED:

How to drill wood and metal ☐

How to mix concrete ☐

How to join wires ☐

How to saw ☐

How a 12-volt actuator works ☐

What my shoe size is ☐ *Not that epic, really!*

How to tidy your bedroom by just pulling a cord ☐

How a pulley system works ☐

What a nut, bolt and washer does ☐

How to create your own fire vortex ☐

How to connect a 9-volt battery ☐

How to make mega cool wooden structures ☐

How screwdrivers, spanners, pliers and drill bits work ☐

... and loads, loads, loads more amazing stuff! ☐